Pro Linux High Availability Clustering

Sander van Vugt

Apress®

Pro Linux High Availability Clustering

ISBN-13 (pbk): 978-1-4842-0080-3

ISBN-13 (electronic): 978-1-4842-0079-7

Publisher: Heinz Weinheimer
Lead Editor: Louise Corrigan
Technical Reviewers: Menno van Saagsvelt, Lars Marowsky-Brée
Editorial Board: Steve Anglin, Mark Beckner, Ewan Buckingham, Gary Cornell, Louise Corrigan, Jim DeWolf, Jonathan Gennick, Jonathan Hassell, Robert Hutchinson, Michelle Lowman, James Markham, Matthew Moodie, Jeff Olson, Jeffrey Pepper, Douglas Pundick, Ben Renow-Clarke, Dominic Shakeshaft, Gwenan Spearing, Matt Wade, Steve Weiss
Coordinating Editor: Christine Ricketts
Copy Editor: Michael G. Laraque
Compositor: SPi Global
Indexer: SPi Global
Artist: SPi Global
Cover Designer: Anna Ishchenko

Distributed to the book trade worldwide by Springer Science+Business Media New York, 233 Spring Street, 6th Floor, New York, NY 10013. Phone 1-800-SPRINGER, fax (201) 348-4505, e-mail orders-ny@springer-sbm.com, or visit www.springeronline.com. Apress Media, LLC is a California LLC and the sole member (owner) is Springer Science + Business Media Finance Inc (SSBM Finance Inc). SSBM Finance Inc is a Delaware corporation.

For information on translations, please e-mail rights@apress.com, or visit www.apress.com.

Apress and friends of ED books may be purchased in bulk for academic, corporate, or promotional use. eBook versions and licenses are also available for most titles. For more information, reference our Special Bulk Sales–eBook Licensing web page at www.apress.com/bulk-sales.

Any source code or other supplementary materials referenced by the author in this text is available to readers at www.apress.com. For detailed information about how to locate your book's source code, go to www.apress.com/source-code.

Ce livre est dedié à Florence

Contents at a Glance

Contents

About the Author

Sander van Vugt is an independent Linux specialist working out of the Netherlands and serving customers all over the world. He functions as a consultant, specializing in Linux HA projects and performance issues. Sander is also the author of more than 55 books, of which most are on Linux-related subjects. Sander also works as a Linux technical instructor, being certified both in SUSE and Red Hat. You can find additional information about Sander's professional interests and qualifications at www.sandervanvugt.com or from his personal web site at www.sandervanvugt.org.

About the Technical Reviewers

Menno van Saagsvelt works as a senior technical consultant for a company in the Netherlands, providing e-learning solutions for (big) companies (especially "Moodle," on clustered LAMP-stacks).

Between 2004 and 2009, he worked for a television and radio station in Monroe, Louisiana, as an IT specialist. He was responsible for their web site and the infrastructure of their web, mail, proxy servers, and intranet.

Before 2004, Menno worked in the Netherlands as an IT technician for a Dutch Internet service provider.

Lars Marowsky-Brée is a high availability and storage architect with SUSE Linux Products GmbH. He has had a leading role in making the Pacemaker software into what it currently is, and he graciously accepted the role of honorary technical reviewer for this book.

Acknowledgments

A special thanks to the people at Apress, who were willing to accept this project and help me through it. Thanks also to my technical editor, Menno van Saagsvelt, who worked his way through all of the text I submitted.

I also want to express my gratitude to Loïc Devulder, senior Linux System Administrator at PSA Peugeot Citroën, who was willing to read through the entire document and share some of his experiences with the software that is described in this book.

I especially want to thank Lars Marowsky-Brée, cluster and storage architect with SUSE and, as such, responsible for significant parts of the Pacemaker software, who graciously made himself available to review most of the contents of this book and make it significantly better.

Introduction

This book is about high availability (HA) clustering on Linux, a subject that can be overwhelming to administrators who are new to the subject. Although much documentation is already available on the subject, I felt a need to write this book anyway. The most important reason is that I feel there is a lack of integral documentation that focuses on tasks that have to be accomplished by cluster administrators. With this book, I have tried to provide insight into accomplishing all of the tasks that a cluster administrator typically has to deal with.

This means that I'm not only focusing on the clustering software itself but also on setting up the network for redundancy and configuring storage for use in a clustered environment. In an attempt to make this book as useful as possible, I have also included three chapters with use cases, at the end of this book.

When working with HA on Linux, administrators will encounter different challenges. One of these is that even if the core components Corosync and Pacemaker are used on nearly all recent Linux distributions, there are many subtle differences.

Instead of using the same solutions, the two most important enterprise Linux distributions that are offering commercially supported HA also want to guarantee a maximum of compatibility with their previous solutions, to make the transition for their customers as easy as possible, and that is revealed by slight differences. For example, Red Hat uses fencing and SUSE uses STONITH, and even if both do the same thing, they are doing it in a slightly different way. For a cluster administrator, it is important to be acutely aware of these differences, because they may cause many practical problems, most of which I have tried to describe in this book.

It has, however, never been my intention to summarize all solutions. I wanted to write a practical field guide that helps people build real clusters. The difference between these two approaches is that it has never been my intention to provide a complete overview of all available options, commands, resource types, and so on. There is already excellent documentation doing this available on the Web. In this book, I have made choices with the purpose of making cluster configuration as easy as possible for cluster administrators.

An important choice is my preference for the crm shell as a configuration interface. This shell is the default management environment on SUSE Linux clusters and is not included in the Red Hat repositories. It is, however, relatively easy to install this shell by adding one additional repository, and, therefore, I felt no need to cover everything I'm doing in this book from both the crm shell as well as the pcmk shell. This would only make the book twice as long and the price twice at high, without serving a specific purpose.

I hope this book meets your expectations. I have tried to make it as thorough as possible, but I'm always open to feedback. Based on the feedback provided, I will make updates available through my web site: www.sandervanvugt.com. If you have purchased this book, I recommend checking my web site, to see if errata and additions are available. If you encounter anything in this book that requires further explanation, I would much appreciate receiving your comments. Please address these to mail@sandervanvugt.nl, and I will share them with the readership of this book.

I am dedicated to providing you, the reader, with the best possible information, but in a dynamic environment such as Linux clustering, things may change, and different approaches may become available. Please share your feedback with me, and I will do my best to provide all the readers of this book with the most accurate and up-to-date information!

—Sander van Vugt

CHAPTER 1

■ ■ ■

High Availability Clustering and Its Architecture

In this chapter, you'll learn how high availability (HA) clustering relates to other types of clustering. You'll also read about some typical use cases for HA clustering. After a discussion on the general concepts of HA clustering, you'll read about its different components and implementations on Linux.

Different Kinds of Clustering

Roughly speaking, three different kinds of cluster can be distinguished, and all of these three types can be installed on Linux servers.

- *High performance*: Different computers work together to host one or more tasks that require lots of computing resources.

- *Load balancing*: A load balancer serves as a front end and receives requests from end users. The load balancer distributes the request to different servers.

- *High availability*: Different servers work together to make sure that the downtime of critical resources is reduced to a minimum.

High Performance Clusters

A high performance cluster is used in environments that have heavy computing needs. Think of large rendering jobs or complicated scientific calculations that are too big to be handled by one single server. In such a situation, the work can be handled by multiple servers, to make sure it is handled smoothly and in a timely manner.

An approach to high performance clustering is the use of a Single System Image (SSI). Using that approach, multiple machines are treated by the cluster as one, and the cluster just allocates and claims the resources where they are available (Figure 1-1). High performance clustering is used in specific environments, and it is not as widespread as high availability clustering.

1

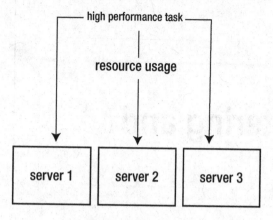

Figure 1-1. *Overview of high performance clustering*

Load Balancing Clusters

Load balancing clusters are typically used in heavy-demand environments, such as very popular web sites. The purpose of a load balancing cluster is to redistribute a task to a server that has resources to handle the task. That seems a bit like high performance clustering, but the difference is that in high performance clusters, typically, all servers are working on the same task, where load balancing clusters take care of load distribution, to get an optimal efficiency in task-handling.

A load balancing cluster consists of two entities: the load balancer and the server farm behind it. The load balancer receives requests from end users and redistributes them to one of the servers that is available in the server farm (Figure 1-2). On Linux, the Linux Virtual Server (LVS) project implements load balancing clusters. HAProxy is another Linux-based load balancer. The load balancers also monitor the availability of servers in the server farm, to decide where resources can be placed. It is also very common to use hardware for load balancing clusters. Vendors like Cisco make hardware devices that are optimized to handle the load as fast and efficiently as possible.

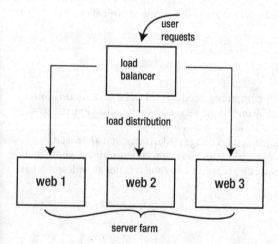

Figure 1-2. *Overview of load balancing clusters*

High Availability Clusters

The goal of a high availability cluster is to make sure that critical resources reach the maximum possible availability. This goal is accomplished by installing cluster software on multiple servers (Figure 1-3). This software monitors the availability of the cluster nodes, and it monitors the availability of the services that are managed by the cluster (in this book, these services are referred to as *resources*). If a server goes down, or if the resource stops, the HA cluster will notice and make sure that the resource is restarted somewhere else in the cluster, so that it can be used again after a minimal interruption. This book is exclusively about HA clusters.

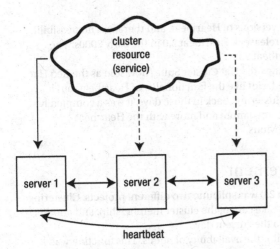

Figure 1-3. *Overview of high availability clusters*

What to Expect from High Availability Clusters

Before starting your own high availability cluster project, it is good to have the appropriate expectations. The most important is to realize that an HA cluster maximizes availability of resources. It cannot ensure that resources are available without interruption. A high availability cluster will act on a detected failure of the resource or the node that is currently hosting the resource. The cluster can be configured to make the resource available as soon as possible, but there will always be some interruption of services.

The topic of this book is HA clustering as it can be used on different Linux distributions. The functionality is often confused with HA functionality, as it is offered by virtualization solutions such as VMware vSphere. It is good to understand what the differences and similarities between these two are.

In VMware vSphere HA, the goal is to make sure that virtual machines are protected against hardware failure. vSphere monitors whether a host or a virtual machine running on a host is still available, and if something happens, it makes sure that the virtual machine is restarted somewhere else. This looks a lot like Linux HA Clustering. In fact, in Chapter 11, you'll even learn how to use Linux HA clustering to create such a solution for KVM Virtual machines.

There is a fundamental difference, though. The HA solution that is offered by your virtualization platform is agnostic on what happens in the virtual machine. That means that if a virtual machine hangs, it will appear as available to the virtualization layer, and the HA solution of your virtualization layer will do nothing. It also is incapable of monitoring the status of critical resources that are running on those virtual machines.

If you want to make sure that your company's vital resources have maximum protection and are restarted as soon as something goes wrong with them, you'll require high availability within the virtual machine. If the virtual machine runs the Windows operating system, you'll need Windows HA. In this book, you'll learn how to set up such an environment for the Linux operating system.

History of High Availability Clustering in Linux

High availability in Linux has a long history. It started in the 1990s as a very simple solution with the name Heartbeat. A Heartbeat cluster basically could do two things: it monitored two nodes (and not more than two), and it was configured to start one or more services on those two nodes. If the node that was currently hosting the resources went down, it restarted the cluster resources on the remaining node.

Heartbeat 2.0 and Red Hat Cluster Suite

There was no monitoring of the resources themselves in the early versions of Heartbeat, and there was no possibility to add more than two nodes to the cluster. This changed with the release of Heartbeat 2.0 in the early 2000s. The current state of Linux HA clustering is based in large part on Heartbeat 2.0.

Apart from Heartbeat, there was another solution for clustering: Red Hat Cluster Suite (now sold as the Red Hat High Availability Add On). The functionality of this solution looked a lot like the functionality of Heartbeat, but it was more sophisticated, especially in the early days of Linux HA clustering. Back in those days, it was a completely different solution, but later, the Red Hat clustering components merged more and more with the Heartbeat components, and in the current state, the differences are not so obvious.

Cluster Membership and Resource Management

An important step in the history of clustering was when Heartbeat 2.0 was split into two different projects. Clustering had become too complex, and therefore, a project was founded to take care of the cluster membership, and another project took care of resource management. This difference exists to the current day.

The main function of the cluster membership layer is to monitor the availability of nodes. This function was first performed by the OpenAIS project, which later merged into the Corosync project. In current Linux clustering, Corosync still is the dominant solution for managing and monitoring node membership. In Red Hat clustering, cman has always been used as the implementation of the cluster membership layer. Cman isn't used often in environments without Red Hat, but in Red Hat environments, it still plays a significant role, as you will learn in Chapter 3.

For resource management, Heartbeat evolved into Pacemaker, which, as its name suggests, was developed to fix everything that Heartbeat wasn't capable of. The core component of Pacemaker is the CRM, or cluster resource manager. This part of the cluster monitors the availability of resources, and if an action has to be performed on resources, it instructs the local resource manager (LRM) that runs on every cluster node to perform the local operation.

In Red Hat, up to Red Hat 6, the resource group manager (rgmanager) was used for managing and placing resources. In Red Hat 6, however, Pacemaker was already offered as an alternative resource manager, and in Red Hat 7, Pacemaker has become the standard for managing resources in Red Hat as well.

The Components That Build a High Availability Cluster

To build a high availability cluster, you'll need more than just a few servers that are tied together. In this section, you'll get an overview of the different components that typically play a role when setting up the cluster. In later chapters, you'll learn in detail how to manage these different components. Typically, the following components are used in most clusters:

- Shared storage
- Different networks
- Bonded network devices
- Multipathing
- Fencing/STONITH devices

It is important to think about how you want to design your cluster and to find out which specific components are required to build the solution you need.

Shared Storage

In a cluster, it's the cluster that decides on which server the shared resources are going to be hosted. On that server, the data and configuration files have to be available. That is why most clusters need shared storage. There are exceptions, though.

Some services don't really have many files that have to be shared, or take care of synchronization of data internally. If your service works with static files only, you might as well copy these files over manually, or set up a file synchronization job that takes care of synchronizing the files in an automated way. But most clusters will have shared storage.

Roughly speaking, there are two approaches to taking care of shared storage. You can use a Network File System (NFS) or a storage area network (SAN). In an NFS, one or more directories are shared over the network. It's an easy way of setting up shared storage, but it doesn't give you the best possible flexibility. That is why many clusters are set up with an SAN.

A SAN is like a collection of external disks that is connected to your server. To access a SAN, you'll need a specific infrastructure. This infrastructure can be Fibre Channel or iSCSI.

Fibre Channel SANs typically are built for the best possible performance. They're using a dedicated SAN infrastructure, which is normally rather expensive. Typically, Fibre Channel SANs costs tens of thousands of dollars, but you get what you pay for: good quality with optimal performance and optimal reliability.

iSCSI SANs were developed to send SCSI commands over an IP network. That means that for iSCSI SAN, a normal Ethernet network can be used. This makes iSCSI a lot more accessible, as anyone can build an iSCSI SAN, based on standard networking hardware. This accessibility gives iSCSI SANs a reputation for being cheap and not so reliable. The contrary is true, though. There are some vendors on the market who develop high-level iSCSI SAN solutions, where everything is optimized for the best possible performance. So, in the end, it doesn't really matter, and both iSCSI and Fibre Channel SANs can be used to offer enterprise-level performance.

Different Networks

You could create a cluster and have all traffic go over the same network. That isn't really efficient, however, because a user who saturates bandwidth on the network would be capable of bringing the cluster down, as the saturated network cluster packets wouldn't come through. Therefore, a typical cluster has multiple network connections (Figure 1-4).

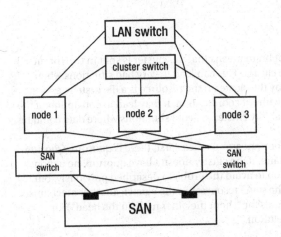

Figure 1-4. *Typical cluster network layout*

First, there is the user network, from which external users access the cluster resources. Next, you would normally have a dedicated network for the cluster protocol packets. This network is to offer the best possible redundancy and ensure that the cluster traffic can come through at all times.

Third, there would typically be a storage network as well. How this storage network is configured depends on the kind of storage that you're using. In a Fibre Channel SAN, the nodes in the cluster would have host bus adapters (HBAs) to connect to the Fibre Channel SAN. On an iSCSI network, the SAN traffic goes over an Ethernet network, and nothing specific is required for the storage network except a dedicated storage network infrastructure.

Bonded Network Devices

To connect cluster nodes to their different networks, you could, of course, use just one network interface. If that interface goes down, the node would lose connection on that network, and the cluster would react. As a cluster is all about high availability, this is not what you typically want to accomplish with your cluster.

The solution is to use network bonding. A network bond is an aggregate of multiple network interfaces. In most configurations, there are two interfaces in a bond. The purpose of network bonding is redundancy: a bond makes sure that if one interface goes down, the other interface will take over. In Chapter 3, you will learn how to set up bonded network interfaces.

Multipathing

When a cluster node is connected to a SAN, there are typically multiple paths the node can follow to see the LUN (logical unit number) on the SAN. This results in the node seeing multiple devices, instead of just one. So, for every path the node has to the LUN, it would receive a device.

In a configuration where a node is connected to two different SAN switches, which, in turn, are connected to two different SAN controllers, there would be four different paths. The result would be that your node wouldn't see only one iSCSI disk, but four. As each of these disks is connected to a specific path, it's not a good idea to use any single one of them. That is why multipath is important.

The multipath driver will detect that the four different disks are, in fact, all just one and the same disk. It offers a specific device, on top of the four different disks, that is going to be used instead. Typically, this device would have a name such as mpatha. The result is that the administrator can connect to mpatha instead of all of the underlying devices, and if one of the paths in the configuration goes down, that wouldn't really matter, as the multipath layer would take care of routing traffic to an interface that still is available. In Chapter 2, you will learn how to set up multipathing.

Fencing/STONITH Devices and Quorum

In a cluster, a situation called split brain needs to be avoided. Split brain means that the cluster is split in two (or more) parts, but both parts think they are the only remaining part of the cluster. This can lead to very bad situations when both parts of the cluster try to host the resources that are offered by the cluster. If the resource is a file system, and multiple nodes try to write to the file system simultaneously and without coordination, it may lead to corruption of the file system and the loss of data. As it is the purpose of a high availability cluster to avoid situations where data could be lost, this must be prevented no matter what.

To offer a solution for split-brain situations, there are two important approaches. First, there is quorum. *Quorum* means "majority," and the idea behind quorum is easy to understand: if the cluster doesn't have quorum, no actions will be taken in the cluster. This by itself would offer a good solution to avoid the problem described previously, but to make sure that it can never happen that multiple nodes activate the same resources in the cluster, another mechanism is used as well. This mechanism is known as STONITH (which stands for "shoot the other node in the head"), or fencing. Both the terms *STONITH* and *fencing* refer to the same solution.

In STONITH, specific hardware is used to terminate a node that is no longer responsive to the cluster. The idea behind STONITH is that before migrating resources to another node in the cluster, the cluster has to confirm that the node in question really is down. To do this, the cluster will send a shutdown action to the STONITH device, which will, in turn, terminate the nonresponsive node. This may sound like a drastic approach, but as it guarantees that no data corruption can ever occur and can clean up certain transient errors (such as a kernel crash), it's not that bad.

When setting up a cluster, you must decide which type of STONITH device you want to use. This is a mandatory decision, as STONITH is mandatory and not optional in Linux HA clusters. The following different types of STONITH devices are available:

- Integrated management boards, such as HP ILO, Dell DRAC ,and IBM RSA

- Power switches that can be managed, such as the APC master device

- Disk-based STONITH, which uses a shared disk device to effectuate the STONITH operation

- Hypervisor-based STONITH, which talks to the hypervisor in a virtualization environment

- Software and demo STONITH solutions (which, in fact, should be avoided at all times)

In Chapter 5, you'll learn how to configure different STONITH and fencing solutions.

Summary

This chapter has given an overview of Linux HA clustering. You've read how HA clustering relates to other types of clustering, and you've learned about the different software components that are used in a typical HA environment. You also have learned about the different parts that are used in high availability clustering, which allows you to properly prepare your high availability environment. In the next chapter, you'll learn how to configure and connect to storage in high availability environments.

CHAPTER 2

■■■

Configuring Storage

Almost all clusters are using shared storage in some way. This chapter is about connecting your cluster to shared storage. Apart from connecting to shared storage, you'll also learn how to set up an iSCSI storage area network (SAN) in your own environment, a subject that is even further explored in Chapter 10. You'll also learn the differences between network attached storage (NAS) and SAN and when to use which. The following topics are covered in this chapter:

- Why most clusters need shared storage
- NAS or SAN?
- iSCSI or Fibre Channel?
- Configuring the LIO iSCSI target
- Connecting to an iSCSI SAN
- Setting up multipathing

Why Most Clusters Need Shared Storage

In an HA cluster, you will make sure that vital resources will be available as much as possible. That means that at one time, your resource may be running on one node, while at another time, the resource may be running on another node. On the other node, the resource will need access to the exact same files, however. That is why shared storage may come in handy.

If your resource only deals with static files, you could do without shared storage. If modifications to the files are only applied infrequently, you could just manually copy the files over, or use a solution such as rsync to synchronize the files to the other nodes in the cluster. If, however, the data is dynamic and changes are frequent, you'll need shared storage.

Typically, a resource uses three different kinds of files. First, there are the binaries that make up the program or service that is offered by the resource. It is best to install these binaries locally on each host. That ensures that every single host in its update procedures will update the required binaries, and it will make sure that the host can still run the application if very bad things are happening to the cluster and you're forced to run everything stand-alone.

The second part of data that is typically used are configuration files. Even if many applications store configuration files by default in the local /etc directory, most applications do have an option to store the configuration files somewhere else. It often is a good idea to put these configuration files on the shared storage. This ensures that your cluster application always has access to the same configuration. In theory, manual synchronization of configuration files between hosts would work as well, but in real life, something always goes wrong, and you risk ending up with two different versions of the same application. So, make sure to put the configuration files on the shared storage and configure your application to access the files from the shared storage and not locally.

The third and most important type of files that applications typically work with is the data files. These normally are a valuable asset for the company, and also, they have to be available from all nodes at all times. That is why the nodes in the cluster are configured to access an SAN disk and the data files are stored on the SAN disk. This ensures that all hosts at all times can access the files from the SAN. The SAN itself is set up in a redundant way, to ensure that the files are highly protected and no interruption of services could occur because of bad configuration. See Figure 2-1 for an overview of this setup.

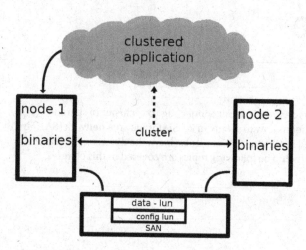

Figure 2-1. *Cluster application file access overview*

NAS or SAN?

When choosing the right solution for shared storage, you must select between network attached storage (NAS) and storage area networks (SAN). Let's discuss some differences and advantages between these two.

NAS

Network attached storage (NAS) is basically a network share that could be offered by any server on the network. In Linux clusters, NAS is typically provided by means of Network File System (NFS) shares, but a Common Internet File System (CIFS) is also a valid option to provide NAS functionality. The advantage of an NAS is that it is simple to set up. There are some other considerations, though.

Typically, NAS services are provided by a server in the network. Now, when setting up a cluster environment, it is of greatest importance to avoid having a single point of failure in the network. So, if you were planning to set up an NFS server to provide for shared storage in your cluster environment, you would have to cluster that as well, to make sure that the shared storage was still available if the primary NFS server dropped. So, you would have to cluster the NFS or CIFS server and make sure that no matter where the services itself were running, it had access to the same files. HA NAS servers that are using NFS or CIFS are commonly applied in HA cluster environments.

A common reason why NAS solutions are used in HA environments is because an NAS gives concurrent file system access, which an SAN won't, unless it is set up with OCFS2 or GFS2 at the client side.

SAN

A storage area network (SAN) is tailored to offer the best possible redundancy, as well as performance to access storage (Figure 2-2). It typically consists of disk arrays. To access these disks, a dedicated network infrastructure is used.

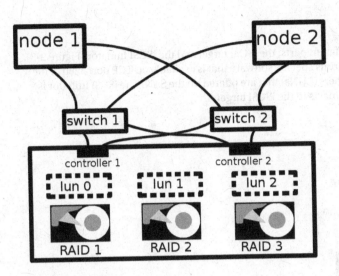

Figure 2-2. *SAN overview*

The disks in the SAN filer are normally set up using RAID. Typically, different RAID arrays are configured to make sure the SAN can survive a crash of several disks simultaneously. On top of those RAID arrays, the logical unit numbers (LUNs) are created. Nodes in the cluster can be authorized to access specific LUNs, which to them will appear as new local disks.

To access the SAN filer, a redundant network infrastructure is normally used. In this infrastructure, most items are double, which means that the nodes have two SAN interfaces that are connected to two SAN switches, which are, in turn, connected to two different controllers on the SAN. All this is to make sure that if something fails, the end user won't notice anything.

iSCSI or Fibre Channel?

Once you have decided to use a storage area network (SAN), the next question arises: is it going to be Fibre Channel or iSCSI? The first SANs that came on the market were Fibre Channel SANs. These were filers that were optimized for the best possible performance and in which a dedicated SAN network infrastructure was used as well. That is because in the time the first SAN solutions appeared, 100 Mbit/s was about the fastest speed available on LAN networks, and compared to the throughput on a local SCSI bus, that was way too slow. Also, networks in those days were using hubs most of the time, which meant that network traffic was dealt with in a rather inefficient way.

However, times have changed, and LAN networks became faster and faster. Gigabit is the minimum standard in current networks, and nearly all hubs have been replaced with switches. In the context of these improved networks, a new standard was created: iSCSI. The idea behind iSCSI is simple: the SCSI packets that are generated and sent on a local disk infrastructure are encapsulated in an IP header to address the SAN.

Fibre Channel SAN has the reputation of being more reliable and faster than iSCSI. This doesn't have to be true, though. Some high-end iSCSI solutions are offered on the market, and if a dedicated iSCSI network is used, where traffic is optimized to handle storage, iSCSI can be as fast and as reliable as Fibre Channel SAN. iSCSI does have an advantage that Fibre Channel SANs don't offer, and that is the relatively easy way that iSCSI SAN solutions can be created. In this chapter, for example, you will learn how to set up an iSCSI SAN yourself.

Another alternative to implement Fibre Channel technology without the need to purchase expensive Fibre Channel hardware is to use Fibre Channel over Ethernet (FCoE). This solution allows Fibre Channel to use 10 Gigabit Ethernet (or faster), while preserving the Fibre Channel protocol. FCoE solutions are available in the major Linux distributions.

Understanding iSCSI

In an iSCSI configuration, you're dealing with two different parts: the iSCSI target and the iSCSI initiator (Figure 2-3). The iSCSI target is the storage area network (SAN). It runs specific software that is available on TCP port 3260 of the SAN and that provides access to the logical unit numbers (LUNs) that are offered on the SAN. The iSCSI initiator is software that runs on the nodes in the cluster and connects to the iSCSI target.

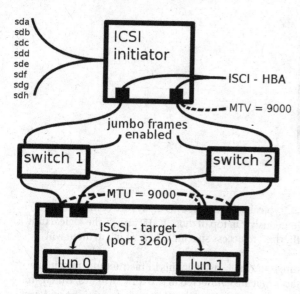

Figure 2-3. *iSCSI overview*

To connect to the iSCSI target, a dedicated SAN network is used. It normally is a regular Ethernet network, but configured in a specific way. To start with, the network is redundant. That means that two different network interfaces on the cluster nodes connect to two different switches, which in turn connect to two different controllers on the SAN that each are accessible by two different network interfaces as well. That means that no less than four different paths exist to access the LUNs that are shared on the SAN. That leads to a situation where every LUN risks being seen four times by the cluster nodes. You'll read more about this in the section about multipathing later in this chapter.

On the SAN network, some specific optimizations can be applied as well. Optimization begins on the cluster nodes, where the administrator can choose to select, not ordinary network cards, but iSCSI host bus adapters (HBAs). These are smart network cards that have been produced to handle iSCSI traffic in the most optimal way. They have their maximum packet size on the Ethernet level set to an MTU of 9000 bytes, to make sure the traffic is handled as fast as possible, and they often use an iSCSI offload engine to handle the iSCSI traffic even more efficiently. However, iSCSI HBAs have become less popular and tend to be replaced by fast network interface cards (NICs).

Configuring the LIO iSCSI Target

There are many different vendors on the market that make iSCSI solutions, but you can also set up iSCSI on Linux. The Linux-IO (LIO) Target is the most common iSCSI target for Linux on recent distributions (Figure 2-4). You will find it on all recent distributions. On SUSE Linux Enterprise Server 12, for instance, you can easily set it up from the YaST management utility. On other distributions, you might find the targetcli utility to configure the iSCSI target. Of course, when setting up a single iSCSI target, you must realize that this can be a single point of failure. Later in this chapter, you'll learn how to set up iSCSI targets in a redundant way.

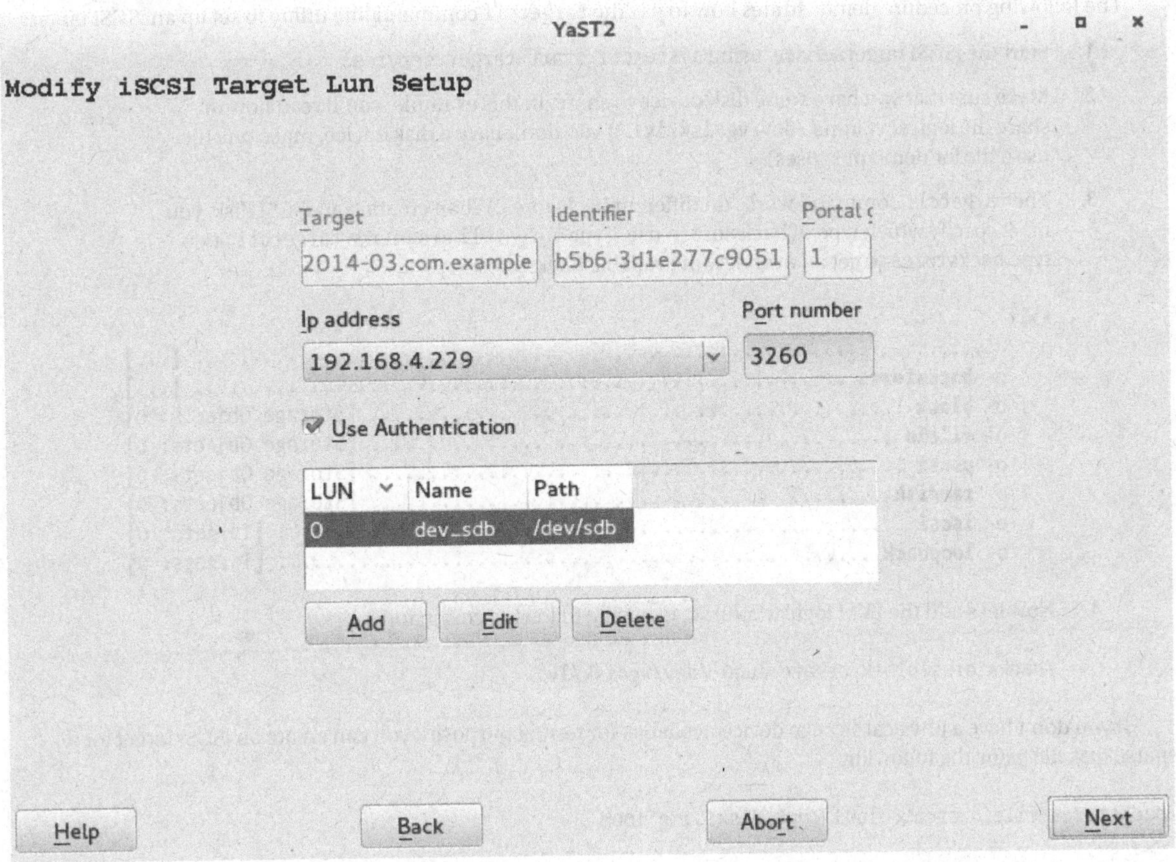

```
                                    YaST2                              -   □   ×

Modify iSCSI Target Lun Setup


            Target               Identifier              Portal ⟨

            2014-03.com.example  b5b6-3d1e277c9051      1

            Ip address                          Port number

            192.168.4.229                  ∨    3260


                 ☑ Use Authentication
            ─────────────────────────────────────────────────

            LUN   ∨  Name      Path
            0        dev_sdb   /dev/sdb



               Add          Edit       Delete



   Help              Back             Abort            Next
```

Figure 2-4. *Setting up the LIO Target from SUSE YaST*

When setting up a target, you must specify the required components. These include the following:

- *Storage device*: This is the storage device that you're going to create. If you're using Linux as the target, it makes sense to use LVM logical volumes as the underlying storage device, because they are so flexible. But you can choose other storage devices as well, such as partitions, complete hard disks, or sparse files.

- *LUN ID*: Every storage device that is shared with an iSCSI target is shared as a LUN, and every LUN needs a unique ID. A LUN ID is like a partition ID; the only requirement is that it has to be unique. There's nothing wrong selecting subsequent numeric LUN IDs for this purpose.

- *Target ID*: If you want to authorize targets to specific nodes, it makes sense to create different targets where every target has its own target ID, also known as the Internet Qualified Name (IQN). From the iSCSI client you need the target ID to connect, so make sure the target ID makes sense and makes it easy for you to recognize a specific target.

- *Identifier*: The identifier helps you to further identify specific iSCSI targets.

- *Port number*: This is the TCP port the target will be listening on. By default, port 3260 is used for this purpose.

The following procedure demonstrates how to use the `targetcli` command line utility to set up an iSCSI target:

1. Start the iSCSI target service, using `systemctl start target.service`.

2. Make sure that you have some disk device to share. In this example, you'll read how to share the logical volume /dev/vgdisk/lv1. If you don't have a disk device, make one (or use a file for demo purposes).

3. The `targetcli` command works on different backstores. When creating an iSCSI disk, you must specify which type of backstore to use. Type `targetcli` to start the `targetcli` and type `backstores` to get an overview of available backstores.

```
/>ls
o- / ........................................................... [...]
  o- backstores ............................................... [...]
  | o- block ...................................... [Storage Objects: 0]
  | o- fileio ..................................... [Storage Objects: 0]
  | o- pscsi ...................................... [Storage Objects: 0]
  | o- ramdisk .................................... [Storage Objects: 0]
  o- iscsi ............................................... [Targets: 0]
  o- loopback ............................................ [Targets: 0]
```

4. Now let's add the LVM logical volume, using the following command:

```
/backstores/block create lun0 /dev/vgdisk/lv1
```

If you don't have a physical storage device available, for testing purposes, you can create an iSCSI target for a sparse disk file using the following:

```
/backstores/fileio create lun1 /opt/disk1.img 100M
```

5. At this point, if you type `ls` again, you'll see the LUN you've just created.

```
/>ls
o- / ........................................................... [...]
  o- backstores ............................................... [...]
  | o- block ...................................... [Storage Objects: 1]
  | | o- lun0 ............. [/dev/vgdisk/lv1 (508.0MiB) write-thru deactivated]
  | o- fileio ..................................... [Storage Objects: 0]
  | o- pscsi ...................................... [Storage Objects: 0]
  | o- ramdisk .................................... [Storage Objects: 0]
  o- iscsi ............................................... [Targets: 0]
  o- loopback ............................................ [Targets: 0]
```

6. Now you need to define the target itself.

```
/> /iscsi create
Created target iqn.2003-01.org.linux-iscsi.localhost.x8664:sn.9d07119d8a12.
Created TPG 1.
```

7. Type cd. It gives an interface that shows all currently existing objects, from which you can select the object you want to use with the arrow keys.

```
o- / ......................................................................[...]
  o- backstores ...........................................................[...]
  | o- block ..............................................[Storage Objects: 1]
  | | o- lun0 ............[/dev/vgdisk/lv1 (508.0MiB) write-thru deactivated]
  | o- fileio .............................................[Storage Objects: 0]
  | o- pscsi ..............................................[Storage Objects: 0]
  | o- ramdisk ............................................[Storage Objects: 0]
  o- iscsi ..........................................................[Targets: 1]
  | o- iqn.2003-01.org.linux-iscsi.localhost.x8664:sn.9d07119d8a12 ...[TPGs: 1]
  |   o- tpg1 ............................................[no-gen-acls, no-auth]
  |     o- acls ...........................................................[ACLs: 0]
  |     o- luns ...........................................................[LUNs: 0]
  |     o- portals .......................................................[Portals: 0]
  o- loopback .......................................................[Targets: 0]
```

Use the arrow keys to select the tpg1 object that you've just created.

8. Now, type portals/ create to create a portal with default settings.

```
/iscsi/iqn.20...119d8a12/tpg1> portals/ create
Using default IP port 3260
Binding to INADDR_ANY (0.0.0.0)
Created network portal 0.0.0.0:3260.
```

9. Now, you can actually assign the LUN to the portal.

```
/iscsi/iqn.20...119d8a12/tpg1> luns/ create /backstores/block/lun0
Created LUN 0.
```

10. And if you want to, limit access to the LUN for a specific iSCSI initiator, using the IQN of that iSCSI initiator (typically, you can get the IQN from the /etc/iscsi/initiatorname file).

```
acls/ create iqn.2014-03.com.example:123456789
```

11. Use cd / and ls to view the current settings.

```
/>ls
o- / ........................................................................[...]
  o- backstores ..............................................................[...]
  | o- block ..................................................[Storage Objects: 1]
  | | o- lun0 ............... [/dev/vgdisk/lv1 (508.0MiB) write-thru activated]
  | o- fileio .................................................[Storage Objects: 0]
  | o- pscsi ..................................................[Storage Objects: 0]
  | o- ramdisk ................................................[Storage Objects: 0]
  o- iscsi .......................................................[Targets: 1]
  | o- iqn.2003-01.org.linux-iscsi.localhost.x8664:sn.9d07119d8a12 ... [TPGs: 1]
  |   o- tpg1 ...............................................[no-gen-acls, no-auth]
  |     o- acls ...........................................................[ACLs: 0]
```

```
        |      o- luns ................................................... [LUNs: 1]
        |      | o- lun0 .......................... [block/lun0 (/dev/vgdisk/lv1)]
        |      o- portals ............................................. [Portals: 1]
        |          o- 0.0.0.0:3260 ...................................... [OK]
        o- loopback ..................................................... [Targets: 0]
```

12. And write the configuration and exit.

```
/>saveconfig
Last 10 configs saved in /etc/target/backup.
Configuration saved to /etc/target/saveconfig.json
/>exit
Global pref auto_save_on_exit=true
Last 10 configs saved in /etc/target/backup.
Configuration saved to /etc/target/saveconfig.json
```

13. At this point, you have a working iSCSI target. The next section teaches you how to connect to it.

Connecting to an iSCSI SAN

Once your storage area network (SAN) is up and running, you can connect to it. Connecting to an iSCSI SAN works the same, no matter what kind of SAN you're using. To connect to the SAN, you'll use the iscsiadm command. Before you can use it efficiently, this command needs a bit of explanation. Some Linux distributions offer a solution to make client configuration easy. On SUSE, this module is offered from the YaST management utility.

The iscsiadm command has different modes. Each of the modes is used at a different stage in handling the iSCSI connection. As an administrator, you'll commonly use the following modes:

- discoverydb, or discovery: This mode is used to query an iSCSI target and find out which targets it is offering.

- node: This is the mode you'll need to log in to a specific iSCSI target.

- session: In this mode, you can get information on current sessions or establish a new session to a target you're already connected to.

- iface and host: These modes allow you to specify how you want to connect to a specific target. The difference between iface and host is discussed in more detail later.

When working with iSCSI, you must also know that it doesn't really have you modify configuration files. To establish a connection, you'll just log in to the iSCSI target. This automatically creates some configuration files for you, and these configuration files are persistent. That means that after a reboot, your server will automatically remember its last iSCSI connections. This makes sense, because it is likely that your server has to connect to the same disks again after a reboot. For the administrator, it means that you have to be aware of the configuration, and in some cases, you have to apply additional operations to remove an iSCSI connection that is no longer needed. Now, let's have a look at how to create a new session with an iSCSI target.

Before using the iscsiadm command to connect to an iSCSI target, you have to make sure that the supporting modules are loaded. Typically, you do that by starting the iSCSI client-support script. The names of these scripts differ among the various distributions. Assuming that the name of the service script is iscsi.service, use systemctl start iscsi.service; systemctl enable iscsi.service (service iscsi start; chkconfig iscsi on on a

System-V server). To make sure all prerequisites are loaded, you can type lsmod | grep iscsi before continuing. The result should look like the following:

```
node1:/etc/init.d # lsmod | grep iscsi
iscsi_tcp                18375   1
libiscsi_tcp             20820   1 iscsi_tcp
libiscsi                 53181   2 iscsi_tcp,libiscsi_tcp
scsi_transport_iscsi     57581   3 iscsi_tcp,libiscsi
scsi_mod                 231658  12 sd_mod,iscsi_tcp,libiscsi,scsi_transport_iscsi,
sg,sr_mod,scsi_dh_rdac,scsi_dh_emc,scsi_dh_hp_sw,scsi_dh_alua,scsi_dh,libata
```

Step 1: discovery Mode

To start with, you must discover what the iSCSI target has to offer. To do this, use iscsiadm --mode discovery --type sendtargets --portal 192.168.1.125:3260 --discover. This command gives back the names of the iSCSI targets it has found.

```
iscsiadm --mode discovery --type sendtargets --portal 192.168.1.125:3260 --discover
192.168.1.125:3260,1 iqn.2014-03.com.example:HAcluster
192.168.1.125:3260,1 iqn.2014-01.com.example:kiabi
```

The command you've just issued doesn't just show you the names of the targets, it also puts them in the iSCSI configuration that is in $ISCSI_ROOT/send_targets. ($ISCSI_ROOT is /etc/iscsi on SUSE and /var/lib/iscsi on Red Hat.) Based on that information, you can already use the -P option to print information that is stored about the current mode on your server. The -P option is followed by a print level, which is like a debug level. All modes support 0 and 1; some modes support more elevated print levels as well.

```
node1:/etc/iscsi/send_targets # iscsiadm --mode discoverydb -P 1
SENDTARGETS:
DiscoveryAddress: 192,3260
DiscoveryAddress: 192.168.178.125,3260
DiscoveryAddress: 192.168.1.125,3260
Target: iqn.2014-01.com.example:kiabi
        Portal: 192.168.1.125:3260,1
                Iface Name: default
Target: iqn.2014-03.com.example:HAcluster
        Portal: 192.168.1.125:3260,1
                Iface Name: default
iSNS:
No targets found.
STATIC:
No targets found.
FIRMWARE:
No targets found.
```

In the preceding example, you used the SENDTARGETS discovery type. Depending on your SAN environment, other discovery types are available as well.

- iSNS allows you to set up an iSNS server, which centrally registrates iSCSI targets.

- firmware is a mode that is used on hardware iSCSI adapters that are capable of discovering iSCSI targets from the firmware.

- SLP is not implemented currently.

Step 2: node Mode

Based on the output of the former command, you will know the IQN names of the targets. You'll need these in the next command, in which you're going to log in to the target to actually create the connection. To log in, you'll use the node mode. *Node* in iSCSI terminology means the actual connection that is established between an iSCSI target and a specific portal. The portal is the IP address and the port number that have to be used to make a connection to the iSCSI target. Now, take a look at the output from the previous discoverydb command, where information was displayed in print level 1. This command shows that two different addresses were discovered where the iSCSI target port is listening, but only one of these addresses has actual associated targets, which can be reached by means of the portals that are listed. This immediately explains why the command in the following code listing fails. Even if the iSCSI port is actually listening on the IP address that is mentioned, there is no target nor portal available on that IP address.

```
node1:/etc/iscsi/send_targets # iscsiadm --mode node --targetname iqn.2014-01.com.example:HAcluster
--portal 192.168.178.125:3260 --login
iscsiadm: No records found
```

Now let's try again on the IP address, to which the iSCSI target is actually connected.

```
node1:/etc/init.d # iscsiadm --mode node --targetname iqn.2014-03.com.example:b36d96e3-9136-44a3-
8bc9-78bd2754a137
--portal 192.168.122.1:3260 --login
Logging in to [iface: default, target: iqn.2014-03.com.example:b36d96e3-9136-44a3-8bc9-78bd2754a137,
portal: 192.168.122.1,3260] (multiple)
Login to [iface: default, target: iqn.2014-03.com.example:b36d96e3-9136-44a3-8bc9-78bd2754a137,
portal: 192.168.122.1,3260] successful.
```

As you can see, because you came in through the right portal this time, you'll get a connection. And as, in this case, the iSCSI target is bound to IP address 0.0.0.0, you'll get a multiple connection, one for each IP address.

At this point, you can verify the connection. An easy way to do that is by using the lsscsi command.

```
node1:/etc/init.d # lsscsi
[0:0:0:0]    cd/dvd   QEMU    QEMU DVD-ROM    0.15   /dev/sr0
[2:0:0:0]    disk     IET     VIRTUAL-DISK    0      /dev/sda
```

As you can see, a virtual disk /dev/sda of the disk type IET has been added. You are now connected to the iSCSI target! If the iSCSI supporting service is enabled in your run levels, the iSCSI connection will also automatically be reestablished while rebooting.

To automatically reestablish all iSCSI sessions, the iSCSI initiator writes its known configuration to $ISCSI-ROOT/nodes. In this directory, you'll find a subdirectory with the name of the target's IQN as its name. In this subdirectory you'll also find a subdirectory for each of the portals the server is connected to, and in that subdirectory, you'll find the default file, containing the settings that are used to connect to the iSCSI target.

```
node1:/etc/iscsi/nodes # ls
iqn.2014-03.com.example:b36d96e3-9136-44a3-8bc9-78bd2754a137
node1:/etc/iscsi/nodes # cd iqn.2014-03.com.example\:b36d96e3-9136-44a3-8bc9-78bd2754a137/
node1:/etc/iscsi/nodes/iqn.2014-03.com.example:b36d96e3-9136-44a3-8bc9-78bd2754a
137 # ls
192.168.122.1,3260,1   192.168.178.36,3260,1
```

```
node1:/etc/iscsi/nodes/iqn.2014-03.com.example:b36d96e3-9136-44a3-8bc9-78bd2754a
137 # cd 192.168.122.1,3260,1/
node1:/etc/iscsi/nodes/iqn.2014-03.com.example:b36d96e3-9136-44a3-8bc9-78bd2754a
137/192.168.122.1,3260,1 # ls
default
```

This configuration ensures that you'll reestablish the exact same iSCSI sessions when rebooting.

Step 3: Managing the iSCSI Connection

Now that you've used the `iscsiadm --mode node` command to make a connection, there are different things that you can do to manage that connection. To start with, let's have a look at the current connection information, using `iscsiadm --mode node -P 1`. The following gives a summary of the current target connections that are existing:

```
node1:~ # iscsiadm --mode node -P 1
Target: iqn.2014-03.com.example:b36d96e3-9136-44a3-8bc9-78bd2754a137
        Portal: 192.168.178.36:3260,1
                Iface Name: default
        Portal: 192.168.122.1:3260,1
                Iface Name: default
```

To get a bit more information about your current setting, including the performance parameters that have been defined in the default file for each session, you can use `iscsiadm --mode session -P 1`, as follows:

```
node1:~ # iscsiadm --mode session -P 2
Target: iqn.2014-03.com.example:b36d96e3-9136-44a3-8bc9-78bd2754a137
        Current Portal: 192.168.122.1:3260,1
        Persistent Portal: 192.168.122.1:3260,1
                *********
                Interface:
                *********
                Iface Name: default
                Iface Transport: tcp
                Iface Initiatorname: iqn.1996-04.de.suse:01:77766ea5aae2
                Iface IPaddress: 192.168.122.130
                Iface HWaddress: <empty>
                Iface Netdev: <empty>
                SID: 1
                iSCSI Connection State: LOGGED IN
                iSCSI Session State: LOGGED_IN
                Internal iscsid Session State: NO CHANGE
                *********
                Timeouts:
                *********
                Recovery Timeout: 120
                Target Reset Timeout: 30
                LUN Reset Timeout: 30
                Abort Timeout: 15
```

```
*****
CHAP:
*****
username: <empty>
password: ********
username_in: <empty>
password_in: ********
************************
Negotiated iSCSI params:
************************
HeaderDigest: None
DataDigest: None
MaxRecvDataSegmentLength: 262144
MaxXmitDataSegmentLength: 8192
FirstBurstLength: 65536
MaxBurstLength: 262144
ImmediateData: Yes
InitialR2T: Yes
MaxOutstandingR2T: 1
```

Disconnecting an iSCSI Session

As mentioned previously, iSCSI is set up to reestablish all sessions on reboot of the server. If your configuration changes, you might have to remove the configuration. To do this, you'll have to remove the session information. To start with, you must disconnect, which also means that the connection is gone from the iSCSI target server perspective. To disconnect a session, you'll use `iscsiadm --mode node --logout`. This disconnects you from all iSCSI disks, which allows you to do maintenance on the iSCSI storage area network. If, after a reboot, you also want the iSCSI sessions not to be reestablished automatically, the easiest approach is to remove the entire contents of the $ISCSI_ROOT/node directory. As on a reboot, the iSCSI service won't find any configuration; you'll be able to start all over again.

Setting Up Multipathing

Typically, the storage area network (SAN) topology is set up in a redundant way. That means that the connection your server has to storage will survive a failure of a controller, disk, network connection, or anything on the SAN. It also means that if you're connecting to the SAN over multiple connections, the logical unit numbers (LUNs) on the SAN will be presented multiple times. If there are four different paths to your LUNs, on the connected node, you'll see /dev/sda, /dev/sdb, and /dev/sdc, as well as /dev/sdd, all referring to the same device.

As all of the /dev/sd devices are bound to a specific path, you shouldn't connect to either of them. If the specific path you're connected to at that moment would fail, you would lose your connection. That is why multipath was invented.

Multipath is a driver that is loaded and that analyzes all of the storage devices. It will find that the devices /dev/sda, /dev/sdb, /dev/sdc, and /dev/sdd are all referring to the same LUN, and, therefore, it will create a specific device that you can connect to instead. Let's have a look at what this looks like on an example server.

To start with, the `iscsiadm -m session -P 1` command shows that two different connections to the SAN exist, using different interfaces and different IP addresses.

```
[root@apache2 ~]# iscsiadm -m session -P 1
Target: iqn.2001-05.com.equallogic:0-8a0906-48578f104-b07002fe41053218-sharedmoodle2
        Current Portal: 192.168.50.126:3260,1
        Persistent Portal: 192.168.50.121:3260,1
                *********
                Interface:
                *********
                Iface Name: p1p1
                Iface Transport: tcp
                Iface Initiatorname: iqn.1994-05.com.redhat:33dbb91a277a
                Iface IPaddress: 192.168.50.103
                Iface HWaddress: <empty>
                Iface Netdev: p1p1
                SID: 1
                iSCSI Connection State: LOGGED IN
                iSCSI Session State: LOGGED_IN
                Internal iscsid Session State: NO CHANGE
        Current Portal: 192.168.50.16:3260,1
        Persistent Portal: 192.168.50.121:3260,1
                *********
                Interface:
                *********
                Iface Name: p1p2
                Iface Transport: tcp
                Iface Initiatorname: iqn.1994-05.com.redhat:33dbb91a277a
                Iface IPaddress: 192.168.50.198
                Iface HWaddress: <empty>
                Iface Netdev: p1p2
                SID: 2
                iSCSI Connection State: LOGGED IN
                iSCSI Session State: LOGGED_IN
                Internal iscsid Session State: NO CHANGE
```

When using lsscsi on that host, you can see that there's a /dev/sdb and a /dev/sdc. So, in this case, there are two different paths to the SAN.

```
[root@apache2 ~]# iscsiadm -m session -P 1
Target: iqn.2001-05.com.equallogic:0-8a0906-48578f104-b07002fe41053218-sharedmoodle2
        Current Portal: 192.168.50.126:3260,1
        Persistent Portal: 192.168.50.121:3260,1
                *********
                Interface:
                *********
                Iface Name: p1p1
                Iface Transport: tcp
                Iface Initiatorname: iqn.1994-05.com.redhat:33dbb91a277a
                Iface IPaddress: 192.168.50.103
                Iface HWaddress: <empty>
                Iface Netdev: p1p1
```

```
            SID: 1
            iSCSI Connection State: LOGGED IN
            iSCSI Session State: LOGGED_IN
    Internal iscsid Session State: NO CHANGE
    Current Portal: 192.168.50.16:3260,1
            Persistent Portal: 192.168.50.121:3260,1
            *********
            Interface:
            *********
            Iface Name: p1p2
            Iface Transport: tcp
            Iface Initiatorname: iqn.1994-05.com.redhat:33dbb91a277a
            Iface IPaddress: 192.168.50.198
            Iface HWaddress: <empty>
            Iface Netdev: p1p2
            SID: 2
            iSCSI Connection State: LOGGED IN
            iSCSI Session State: LOGGED_IN
            Internal iscsid Session State: NO CHANGE
```

On this server, the multipath driver is loaded. To check the current topology, you can use the multipath -l command.

```
[root@apache2 ~]# multipath -l
mpatha (36090a048108f574818320541fe0270b0) dm-2 EQLOGIC,100E-00
size=700G features='0' hwhandler='0' wp=rw
|-+- policy='round-robin 0' prio=0 status=active
| `- 7:0:0:0 sdb 8:16 active undef running
`-+- policy='round-robin 0' prio=0 status=enabled
  `- 8:0:0:0 sdc 8:32 active undef running
```

As you can see, a new device has been created, with the name mpatha. This device is created in the /dev/mapper directory on the cluster node that runs the multipath service. You can also see that it is using round-robin to connect to the underlying devices sdb and sdc. Of these, one has the status set to active, and the other has the status set to enabled.

At this point, the cluster node would address the SAN storage through the /dev/mapper/mpatha device. If during the connection one of the underlying paths failed, it wouldn't really matter. The multipath driver automatically switches to the remaining device.

/etc/multipath.conf

When starting the multipath service, a configuration file is used. In this configuration file, different settings with regard to the multipath device can be specified. In the following listing, you can see what the contents of the file might look like:

```
#blacklist {
#       wwid 26353900f02796769
#       devnode "^(ram|raw|loop|fd|md|dm-|sr|scd|st)[0-9]*"
#       devnode "^hd[a-z]"
#}
```

```
#multipaths {
#       multipath {
#              wwid                   3600508b4000156d700012000000b0000
#              alias                  yellow
#              path_grouping_policy   multibus
#              path_checker           readsector0
#              path_selector          "round-robin 0"
#              failback               manual
#              rr_weight              priorities
#              no_path_retry          5
#       }
#       multipath {
#              wwid                   1DEC_____321816758474
#              alias                  red
#       }
#}
#devices {
#       device {
#              vendor                 "COMPAQ"
#              product                "HSV110 (C)COMPAQ"
#              path_grouping_policy   multibus
#              getuid_callout         "/lib/udev/scsi_id --whitelisted --device=/dev/%n"
#              path_checker           readsector0
#              path_selector          "round-robin 0"
#              hardware_handler       "0"
#              failback               15
#              rr_weight              priorities
#              no_path_retry          queue
#       }
#       device {
#              vendor                 "COMPAQ"
#              product                "MSA1000"
#              path_grouping_policy   multibus
#       }
#}
#
defaults {
        udev_dir               /dev
        find_multipaths        yes
        user_friendly_names    yes
}

multipaths {
        multipath {
                wwid 36090a048108f574818320541fe0270b0
                alias mpatha
        }
}
```

In this preceding listing, different parameters are used. To start with, there is a blacklist section (which is commented out). In this section, you can exclude specific devices. This makes sense, if you're using SAN hardware that has its own multipath drivers and shouldn't use the generic Linux multipath driver. While blacklisting, you can use a World Wide ID (WWID) to refer to the specific device that should be excluded. Also, in the blacklist section, you can see a list of devnodes that are excluded. This list typically contains the local devices, as you wouldn't want to do any multipathing on local devices.

At the end of the configuration file, you can see the settings that actually are effective in this configuration. It starts with the defaults, indicating which directory to use to create the device files for multipath devices. Next, it instructs the multipath driver to use user-friendly names. Another important part is where an alias is set. This alias is based on the WWID, which is the unique ID for a multipath device. If you do nothing, you'll just have a generic device mapper device name like /dev/dm-1, referring to the multipath device.

Because the /dev/dm-* names are set locally and can be different on different nodes in the cluster, they may never be used. This is why a WWID is used instead, to set an alias for the multipath device. To find out which WWID to use, apply the following procedure:

1. Make sure all of the SAN connections are operational.

2. Start the multipath service, using a command such as `systemctl start multipath.service` (it might be different on your distribution).

3. Type `multipath -l` to find the current WWIDs and identify which specific ID is used on which specific LUNs.

4. Decide which alias to use and create the configuration in /etc/multipath.conf.

Specific Use Cases for Multipath

Setting up multipath on a storage area network (SAN) that has two different interfaces is easy. Some modern SANs, however, use virtual interfaces on the SAN, in which the SAN handles the redundancy internally. In such a configuration, you may connect your cluster node to the SAN over redundant paths, but it would get the same information on both paths, with the result that your cluster node doesn't see that there are actually two paths. On a Fibre Channel SAN, this is typically dealt with by the HBA, and there won't be any problem. On an iSCSI SAN, however, it may lead to a situation in which the second path is simply ignored. So, there would be physically multiple paths, of which only the first path is used. That would mean that connection to storage is lost, if that specific path goes down. To deal with these specific cases, you'll have to set up the iSCSI connections in a specific way.

Let's have a look at what exactly the problem is. In Figure 2-5, you see a schematic overview of the configuration. The situation is easily simulated in a test environment. Just make sure a cluster node has two physical interfaces with different IP addresses in the same IP subnet. Next, try to connect to the SAN using the `iscsiadm` command, as described above, with `iscsiadm -m discoverydb --type discovery --portal 192.168.50.121:3260 --discover` and `iscsiadm -m node --targetname iqn.2013-03.com.example:apache --portal 192.168.50.121:3260 --login`. You'll notice that you just have one established session.

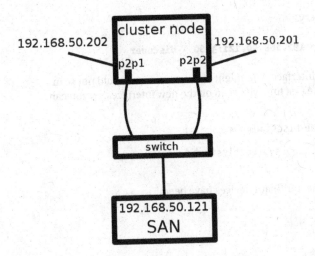

Figure 2-5. Partial multipathing configuration

The following procedure describes how to establish the iSCSI connection in the right way, allowing you to work on a truly redundant configuration.

1. Log out from all existing sessions: iscsiadm --mode node --targetname iqn.2013-03. com.example:apache --portal 192.168.50.121:3260 --logout

2. Stop the iscsid service and remove all current session configuration files: systemctl stop iscsid.service; rm -rf $ISCSI_ROOT/nodes $ISCSI_ROOT/ifaces

3. Now, you have to define different interfaces in iSCSI. This tells iSCSI that each interface should be dealt with separately.

    ```
    iscsiadm --mode iface --interface p2p1 -o new
    iscsiadm --mode iface --interface p2p2 -o new
    ```

4. After defining the interfaces, you must write the interface settings. These settings are written to the $ISCSI_ROOT/ifaces directory and allow iSCSI to distinguish between the interfaces.

    ```
    iscsiadm --mode iface --interface p2p1 -o update --name
    \ iface.net_ifacename --value=p2p1
    iscsiadm --mode iface --interface p2p2 -o update --name
    \ iface.net_ifacename --value=p2p2
    ```

5. Before getting operational, you'll have to tell the kernel of each node that it can accept packets that are sent to addresses in the same IP network on different interfaces. To prevent spoof attacks, this is off by default, which means that the kernel accepts packets to a specific IP subnet on one interface only. To change this behavior, add the following line to the end of /etc/sysctl.conf and reboot:

    ```
    net.ipv4.conf.default/rp_filter = 2
    ```

6. After the reboot, you can start the iSCSI discovery.

```
iscsiadm -m discoverydb -t sendtarets -p 192.168.50.121:3260 --discover
```

As a result, you will see two connections, one for each interface. You might also see an error "could not scan /sys/class/iscsi_transport." This error is perfectly normal the first time you scan on the new interfaces, so you can safely ignore it.

7. Now, you can log in to the SAN with the command `iscsiadm -m node -l`.

8. At this point, you can start the multipath driver, using `systemctl start multipathd.service`.

9. If you now type `multipath -l`, you'll see that the multipath devices have been created properly.

Summary

Connecting to shared storage is important in any high availability cluster. In this chapter, you've read about the different kinds of shared storage that are available and how you can connect to them. In particular, you've learned how to connect to an iSCSI SAN, using the `iscsiadm` command. Also, you have learned how to guarantee redundancy on the SAN connections, by using the multipath driver. In the next chapter, you will learn how to set up the lower layers of the cluster.

■ ■ ■

## CHAPTER 3

Configuring the Membership Layer

For nodes to be able to see one another, you have to configure the cluster membership layer. This layer consists of the infrastructure that is used by the nodes for communication, as well as a software layer that has the nodes actually communicate. This chapter explains how to configure the membership layer. The following topics are discussed:

- Configuring the network

- Dealing with multicast

- corosync or cman?

- Configuring corosync

- Configuring cman

Configuring the Network

Before even starting to think about configuration of the software, you'll have to set up the physical network, and there are a few choices to make. First, you must decide which network you want to use. The choices are between using the LAN and using a dedicated cluster network.

For test environments, it is acceptable to send cluster traffic over the LAN. For production networks, you shouldn't. That is because the cluster traffic is sensitive, and important decisions are made, based on the result of the cluster traffic. If packets don't come through, the cluster will draw the conclusion that a node has disappeared, and it will act accordingly. That means that it will terminate the node it doesn't see anymore, by using STONITH, and it will next migrate resources away to a new location. Both involve downtime for the user who's using the resources, and that is why you want a dedicated cluster network.

On the cluster network, you also need protection on the network connection. You don't want the cluster to fail if a network card goes down, or if a cable is disconnected. That's why you want to configure network bonding, also referred to as link aggregation.

In a network bond, one logical interface is created to put two (or more) physical interfaces together. The physical interfaces don't contain any information if they're in a bond; they are just configured as slaves to the bond. It is the boding interface that contains the IP address configuration. So, the clients communicate to the bonding interface, which uses the bonding kernel module to distribute the load over the slave interfaces.

Network Bonding Modes

When configuring network bonding, there are different modes that you can choose from. The default mode is `balance-rr`, a round-robin mode in which network packets are transmitted in sequential order from the first available network interface through the last. This mode provides load balancing as well as fault tolerance. On some SAN filters, round-robin is deprecated, because according to the vendor, it leads to packet loss. In that case, the Link Aggregation Control Protocol (LACP) is often favored. LCAP, however, doesn't work without support on the switch. The advantage of plain round-robin is that it works without any additional configuration.

Table 3-1 gives an overview of the modes that are available when using bonding on Linux.

Table 3-1. Linux Bonding Modes

Mode	Use
balance-rr	This is the round-robin mode in which packets are transmitted in sequential order from the first network interface through the last.
active-backup	In this mode, only one slave is active, and the other slave takes over, if the active slave fails.
balance-xor	A mode that provides load balancing and fault tolerance and in which the same slave is used for each destination MAC address.
broadcast	This mode provides fault tolerance only and broadcasts packets on all slave interfaces.
802.3ad	This is the LACP mode that creates aggregation groups in which the same speed and duplex settings are used on all slaves. It requires additional configuration on the switch.
balance-tlb	In this mode, which is known as adaptive transmit load balancing, a packet goes out, according to load, on each network interface slave. Incoming traffic is received by a designated slave interface.
balance-alb	This works like `balance-tlb` but also load balances incoming packets.

Configuring the Bond Interface

Configuring a bond interface is not too hard, although the exact procedure may be a bit different on a specific Linux distribution. The procedure described here is based on SUSE Linux Enterprise Server 11 and also works on Red Hat Enterprise Linux 12. Networking has changed considerably in the recently released SUSE Linux Enterprise Server 12 and also in Red Hat Enterprise Linux 7. I recommend using SUSE's YaST setup utility or the Red Hat `nm-tui` utility, for setting up bonding in these distributions.

The first step is to create an interface configuration file for the bond. This would typically have the name `ifcfg-bond0`, and you will find it in `/etc/sysconfig/network` (SUSE) or `/etc/sysconfig/network-scripts` (Red Hat). In Listing 3-1, you see what the file may look like.

Listing 3-1. Sample Bond Configuration File

```
san:~ # cat /etc/sysconfig/network/ifcfg-bond0
BONDING_MASTER='yes'
BONDING_MODULE_OPTS='mode=active-backup miimon=100'
BONDING_SLAVE0='eth0'
BONDING_SLAVE1='eth1'
BOOTPROTO='static'
BROADCAST=''
```

```
ETHTOOL_OPTIONS=''
IPADDR='192.168.122.140/24'
MTU=''
NAME=''
NETWORK=''
REMOTE_IPADDR=''
STARTMODE='auto'
USERCONTROL='no'
```

There are a few things to note in this sample file. First, the BONDING-SLAVE lines indicate which network interface is used as slave device. As you can see, in this configuration, there are two interfaces added to the bond.

Another important parameter is BONDING_MODULE_OPTS. Here, the options that are passed to the bonding kernel module are specified. As you can see, the mode is set to active_backup, and the miimon parameter tells the bond how frequently the bonding interface has to be monitored (expressed in milliseconds). If you want to make sure your bond reacts fast, you might consider setting this parameter to 50 milliseconds.

If you have specified the BONDING_SLAVE lines in the bond configuration, you don't have to create any configuration for the interfaces that are assigned to the bond device. Just make sure that no configuration file exists for them, and the bond will work. There's also no need to tell the kernel to load the bonding kernel module. This will be loaded automatically when the bond device is initialized from the network scripts.

If you don't have the BONDING_SLAVE lines in the bond configuration, you have to modify the interface file for each of the intended slave interfaces. (These are the files /etc/sysconfig/network-scripts/ifcfg-eth0 and so on.) In Listing 3-2, you can see what the contents of this file has to look like.

Listing 3-2. Sample Interface File with Bonding Configuration

```
DEVICE=eth0
BOOTPROTO=none
ONBOOT=yes
USERCTL=no
MASTER=bond0
SLAVE=yes
TYPE=Ethernet
```

Dealing with Multicast

Another part of network configuration to consider is multicast support. Multicast is the default communication method, because it is easy to set up. For environments in which multicast cannot be used, unicast is supported as well. Later in this chapter, you'll read how to set up your cluster for unicast. On many networks, this is an issue. In general, if all the cluster nodes are connected to the same physical switch, there are no issues with multicast. On many networks, different switches are connected to one another to create one big broadcast domain. If that is the case, you specifically have to take action, to make sure multicast packets originating from one switch are forwarded to all other switches as well.

The parameter to look at is multicast snooping (also referred to as IGMP snooping). IGMP snooping causes the switch to forward multicast packets only to those switch ports in which a multicast address has been detected. In general, this is good, because it means that all other nodes are not receiving the multicast packet. On networks where switches are interconnected, however, it may cause problems. As cluster nodes by default use multicast to communicate, it will lead to cluster nodes not seeing one another. If this happens, you may consider switching off multicast snooping completely on the switches (which will degrade performance, though).

If your switch is a virtual bridge device, as is commonly used on KVM and Xen virtualized environments, you can modify the multicast_snooping behavior by changing a parameter in the sysfs file system. In /sys/class/net, every bridge that is configured has a subdirectory, for example, /sys/class/net/br0. In this directory, you'll find the bridge/multicast_snooping file, which, by default, has the value 1, to enable multicast snooping. If you're experiencing problems with multicast, change the value of this file to 0, by echoing the value into the file. If that works, you can also try the value 2, which does enable multicast_snooping, but in a smart mode, that is supposed to work also between different switches that are interconnected.

To automate this configuration setting, you should include it somewhere in the boot procedure. You can do this by modifying the /etc/init.d/boot.local file to include the following script lines:

```
# set multicast_snooping
cd /sys/class/net
for i in br*
do
        echo 0 > br$i/bridge/multicast_snooping
done
```

corosync or cman?

In all current HA cluster stacks, corosync is the default solution. That means that you should use corosync in all cases. In some specific situations, however, corosync doesn't work. At the time this was written, that was the case with Red Hat Enterprise Linux 6.X, in which cLVM or GFS2 file systems had to be used. This behavior is expected to change with Red Hat Enterprise Linux 7.X.

Configuring corosync

To create a cluster that is based on Corosync, make sure that the corosync, pacemaker, and crmsh packages are installed. In this section, you'll configure corosync only, but it must be aware of the resource management layer as well, and that is why you want to install the pacemaker while installing the corosync package. To be able to manage the Pacemaker layer later, also install the crmsh environment at this point. The following procedure describes how to set up a base cluster using corosync:

1. Open the file /etc/corosync/corosync.conf in your favorite text editor.

2. Locate the bindnetaddr parameter. This parameter should have as its value the IP address that is used to send the cluster packets. Next, change the nodeid parameter. This is the unique ID for this node that is going to be used on the cluster. To avoid any conflicts with auto-generated node IDs, it's better to manually change the node ID. The last byte of the IP address of this node could be a good choice for the node ID.

3. Find the mcastaddr address. As not all multicast addresses are supported in all situations, make sure the multicast address starts with 224.0.0. (Yes, really, it makes no sense, but some switches can only work with these addresses!) All nodes in the same cluster require the same multicast address here. If you have several clusters, every cluster needs a unique multicast address. The final result will look like Listing 3-3.

Listing 3-3. Example `corosync.conf` Configuration File

```
compatibility: whitetank

aisexec {
        user:           root
        group:          root
}

service {
        ver:            0
        name:           pacemaker
        use_logd:       yes
}

totem {
        version:        2
        token:          5000
        token_retransmits_before_loss_const: 10
        join:           60
        consensus:      6000
        vsftype:        none
        max_messages:   20
        clear_node_high_bit: yes
        secauth:        off
        threads:        0

        interface {
                ringnumber: 0
                bindnetaddr: 192.168.122.130
                mcastaddr: 239.0.0.95
                mcastport: 5405
                ttl: 1
        }
}

logging {
        fileline: off
        to_stderr: no
        to_logfile: no
        to_syslog: yes
        syslog_facility: daemon
        debug: off
        timestamp: off
        logger_subsys {
                subsys: AMF
                debug: off
        }
}

amf {
        mode: disabled
}
```

4. If you're creating the configuration on SUSE, you'll be fine and won't need anything else. On Red Hat, you will have to tell corosync which resource manager is used. That is because on Red Hat, you might be using rgmanager instead. To do this on Red Hat, create a file with the name /etc/corosync/service.d/pcmk, and give it the same contents as in Listing 3-4.

Listing 3-4. Telling corosync to Start the Pacemaker Cluster Manager

```
service {
name: pacemaker
ver: 1
}
END
```

Note that in the sample corosync.conf configuration file from Listing 3-3, there already is a service { } section that tells corosync to load pacemaker. As this section is absent in the sample configuration files on Red Hat, you risk overlooking it.

5. Close the configuration file and write the changes. Now, start the corosync service. SUSE uses the openais service script to do that (that's for legacy reasons). On Red Hat and related distributions, you can just use service corosync start to start the corosync service. Also, make sure the service will automatically restart on reboot of the node, using chkconfig [openais|corosync] on. On SLES 12 and RHEL 7, you'll use systemctl start pacemaker to start the services and systemctl enable pacemaker to make sure it starts automatically.

6. At this point, you have a one-node cluster. As root, run the crm_mon command, to verify that the cluster is operational (see Listing 3-5).

Listing 3-5. Verifying Cluster Operation with crm_mon

```
Last updated: Tue Feb  4 08:42:18 2014
Last change: Tue Feb  4 07:41:00 2014 by hacluster via crmd on node2
Stack: classic openais (with plugin)
Current DC: node2 - partition WITHOUT quorum
Version: 1.1.9-2db99f1
1 Nodes configured, 2 expected votes
0 Resources configured.

Online: [ node2 ]
```

7. At this point, you have a one-node cluster. You now have to get the configuration to the other side as well. To do this, use the command scp /etc/corosync/corosync.conf node1 (in which you need to change the name node1 by the name of your other node). On SLES, the recommended way is to use hac-cluster-join from the new node, which copies over corosync.conf and sets up SSH and other required parameters.

8. Open the file /etc/corosync/corosync.conf on the second node and change the nodeid parameter. Make sure a unique node ID is used, or use automatically configured node IDs (which is the default). Also, change the bindnetaddr line. This should reflect the IP network address that corosync should bind to (and not the IP address).

9. Start and enable the openais service and run crm_mon. You should now see that there are two nodes in the cluster.

Understanding corosync.conf Settings

Now that you have established your first cluster, let's have a look at some of the configuration parts in the corosync.conf file. The first important part is the service section, which you can see in Listing 3-3. In this section, you'll tell corosync what it should load. Instead of putting this configuration in corosync.conf, you can also include it in the /etc/corosync/service.d directory.

In Listing 3-3, you can see that the name of the service to be loaded is set to pacemaker. Apart from that, the use_mgmtd parameter is used to load the management daemon, an interface that is required to use the legacy crm_gui management tool. The parameter use_logd tells the cluster to have its own log process. Both of these parameters are no longer needed in the latest releases of SLES and RHEL.

The important part of the corosync.conf file is the totem section. Here, you define how the protocol should be used. In the totem topology, a cluster ring is used. This ring consists of all the cluster nodes, which pass a token around the ring. The token parameter specifies how much time is allowed for the token to be passed around, expressed in milliseconds. So, by default, the token has five seconds to pass around the ring.

Related to the token parameter is the token_retransmits_before_loss_const parameter. This is the amount of tokens that can be missed before a node is considered to be lost in the cluster. A node will be considered lost if it hasn't been heard from for the token time-out period, so, by default, after five seconds.

The next important part is the declaration of the interfaces. In Listing 3-4, only one interface is declared to use one ring only. If you want cluster traffic to be redundant, you might consider setting up a redundant ring, by including a second interface. If you do, make sure to use a unique multicast address and give the ring number 1. Also, you must set the rrp_mode (redundant ring protocol mode). Set it to active, to make sure that both rings are actively being used. Instead of using rrp, it is a better solution to use bonding on the network interface, which is easier to set up and enables redundancy for other services also.

You could also include a logging section, to further define how logging is handled. Listing 3-6 gives a sample configuration.

Listing 3-6. Sample corosync.conf Logging Section

```
logging {
        fileline: off
        to_stderr: no
        to_logfile: yes
        to_syslog: yes
        logfile: /var/log/cluster/corosync.log
        debug: off
        timestamp: on
}
```

Use these self-explanatory parameters to define how logging should be handled in your cluster.

Networks Without Multicast Support

On some networks, multicast is not supported. If that is the case for your network, the procedure that was described in the previous section did not work. You'll have to create a configuration that is based on the UDPU protocol configuration, to get it working. The most relevant differences with the configuration that was described previously are the following:

- In the interface section, you have to include the addresses of all nodes that are allowed as members on the cluster.

- You no longer need a multicast address.

In Listing 3-7, you can see what a typical unicast cluster configuration would look like.

Listing 3-7. Unicast corosync Cluster Configuration

```
aisexec {
        group:  root
        user:   root
}
service {
        use_mgmtd:      yes
        use_logd:       yes
        ver:    0
        name:   pacemaker
}
totem {
        rrp_mode:       none
        join:   60
        max_messages:   20
        vsftype:        none
        transport:      udpu
        nodeid: 145
        consensus:      6000
        secauth:        off
        token_retransmits_before_loss_const:   10
        token:  5000
        version:        2
        interface {
                bindnetaddr:    192.168.1.0
                member {
                        memberaddr:     192.168.1.144
                }
                member {
                        memberaddr:     192.168.1.145
                }
                mcastport:      5405
                ringnumber:     0
        }
        clear_node_high_bit:    no
}
logging {
        to_logfile:     no
        to_syslog:      yes
        debug:  off
        timestamp:      off
        to_stderr:      no
        fileline:       off
        syslog_facility:        daemon
}
amf {
        mode:   disable
}
```

There are two configuration parameters that need a bit more explanation in Listing 3-7. Also in unicast mode, redundant rings can be used (but consider using bonding instead). And if you want to keep the contents of the corosync.conf file identical on all nodes, you may consider using auto-generated node IDs.

Configuring cman

As mentioned previously, corosync should be the default solution you're using to implement the membership layer. As you will have a hard time using corosync with cLVM and GFS2 shared storage in Red Hat 6.X, on occasion, you also might have to use cman at the membership layer. The following procedure describes how to do this:

1. Install required software.

   ```
   yum install -y cman gfs2-utils gfs2-cluster
   ```

2. Edit /etc/sysconfig/cman and make sure it includes the following line:

   ```
   CMAN_QUORUM_TIMEOUT=0
   ```

3. Create the file /etc/cluster/cluster.conf with the following contents (make sure to replace node names). Note that it does include a fencing "dummy." cman must be able to fence nodes, but if that happens, it must send the fencing instruction to the Pacemaker layer (fencing is discussed in depth in Chapter 5):

   ```
   <?xml version="1.0"?>
   <cluster config_version="1" name="mysql-cluster">
     <logging debug="off"/>
     <clusternodes>
       <clusternode name="mysql1.moodle.hosting.local" nodeid="1">
        <fence>
          <method name="pcmk-redirect">
            <device name="pcmk" port="mysql1.moodle.hosting.local"/>
          </method>
        </fence>
       </clusternode>
       <clusternode name="mysql2.moodle.hosting.local" nodeid="2">
        <fence>
          <method name="pcmk-redirect">
            <device name="pcmk" port="mysql2.moodle.hosting.local"/>
          </method>
        </fence>
       </clusternode>
     </clusternodes>
     <fencedevices>
        <fencedevice name="pcmk" agent="fence_pcmk"/>
     </fencedevices>
   </cluster>
   ```

4. Run `ccs_config_validate` to validate the configuration.

5. Start cman and pacemaker services on both nodes, as follows:

    ```
    service cman start; service pacemaker start
    ```

6. Put both services in the runlevels, as follows:

    ```
    chkconfig cman on; chkconfig pacemaker on
    ```

7. Use `cman_tool` nodes to verify availability of the nodes.

8. Use `crm_mon` to verify availability of the resources.

9. Restart both nodes and use `cman_tool` nodes to verify that all comes up.

Summary

In this chapter, you have learned how to create the cluster membership layer. You first read how to set up network bonding to add protection at the network level. Next you read how to make sure multicast works smoothly in your environment. Following that you read how to set up corosync in either multicast or unicast mode. The last part of this chapter was dedicated to installing cman in Red Hat environments. In the next chapter, you'll learn more about the way Pacemaker is organized and managed.

CHAPTER 4

■ ■ ■

Understanding Pacemaker Architecture and Management

If you really want to be a good cluster administrator, you have to understand the way the Pacemaker resource manager is organized. Understanding architecture is of vital importance for managing Pacemaker, because error messages often are organized around different parts of the Pacemaker architecture, and even tools focus on specific parts of the architecture.

The following topics are covered in this chapter:

- Pacemaker related to other parts of the cluster

- Pacemaker internal components

- Cluster management tools

Pacemaker Related to Other Parts of the Cluster

When building a cluster, it is relevant to know how Pacemaker relates to other parts of the cluster. Figure 4-1 gives an overview.

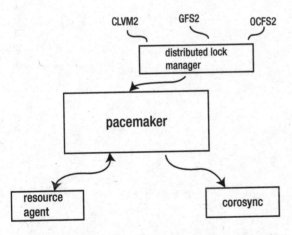

Figure 4-1. *Pacemaker related to other parts of the cluster*

Resource Agents

As you already know, Pacemaker is the part of the cluster that takes care of resource management. To manage resources, resource agents are used. A resource agent is a script that the cluster uses to start, stop, and monitor resources. It can be compared to a systemctl or a runlevel script, but it has been adapted for use in the cluster. It is also the resource agent that defines which properties can be managed by the cluster. As a cluster administrator, it is important to know which properties you can use, before starting to configure resources. Later in this chapter, you will learn how the cluster management tools can help you to analyze which properties are offered by the resource agents.

corosync/cman

As you've already learned, Corosync is the layer that takes care of node membership. You have also seen that it is configured to communicate to Pacemaker. Pacemaker receives updates about changes in cluster membership status, based on which it can initiate certain events, such as resource migration.

The Storage Layer

Pacemaker clusters can be used to manage shared storage devices. For all of these, a distributed lock manager (DLM) is required. This DLM takes care of synchronizing locks on storage devices between nodes, which is especially important if shared storage is involved, such as cLVM2 clustered logical volumes or the GFS2 and OCFS2 clustered file systems. Chapter 7 covers in depth how to configure and manage shared storage in a cluster.

Pacemaker Internal Components

Within the Pacemaker resource manager, different components communicate to one another to decide where the resources should be started. Figure 4-2 gives a schematic overview of the most important part of the Pacemaker internal architecture.

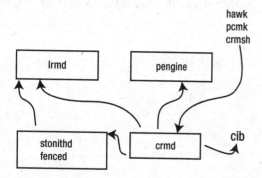

Figure 4-2. *Pacemaker internal architecture*

Cluster Information Base

The heart of the cluster is the Cluster Information Base (CIB). This is the in-memory actual state of the cluster that is continuously synchronized between nodes in the cluster. It is very important to know that as a cluster administrator, you will never directly modify the CIB. For advanced debugging purposes, however, it is a useful source of information.

To understand how the cluster management tools work, it is good to know how the CIB is organized. In Listing 4-1, you see the abbreviated output of the cibadmin -Q command, which dumps the contents of the CIB. The total output of this command in the sample cluster from which it was taken is about ten pages. For readability, I have omitted most of its contents.

Listing 4-1. Partial cibadmin -Q Output

```
[root@mysql2 ~]# cibadmin -Q
<cib epoch="89" num_updates="34" admin_epoch="0" validate-with="pacemaker-1.2" cib-last-written="Thu
Mar 20 16:46:01 2014" update-origin="mysql1.moodle.hosting.local" update-client="crm_resource" crm_
feature_set="3.0.7" have-quorum="1" dc-uuid="mysql2.moodle.hosting.local">
  <configuration>
    <crm_config>
      <cluster_property_set id="cib-bootstrap-options">
        <nvpair id="cib-bootstrap-options-dc-version" name="dc-version" value="1.1.10-14.el6_5.2-
        368c726"/>
        <nvpair id="cib-bootstrap-options-cluster-infrastructure" name="cluster-infrastructure"
        value="classic openais (with plugin)"/>
        <nvpair id="cib-bootstrap-options-expected-quorum-votes" name="expected-quorum-votes" value="2"/>
        <nvpair id="cib-bootstrap-options-last-lrm-refresh" name="last-lrm-refresh" value="1395330310"/>
      </cluster_property_set>
    </crm_config>
    <nodes>
      <node id="mysql2.moodle.hosting.local" uname="mysql2.moodle.hosting.local"/>
      <node id="mysql1.moodle.hosting.local" uname="mysql1.moodle.hosting.local"/>
    </nodes>
    <resources>
      <primitive id="FenceSQ1" class="stonith" type="fence_drac5">
        <instance_attributes id="FenceSQ1-instance_attributes">
          <nvpair name="action" value="reboot" id="FenceSQ1-instance_attributes-action"/>
          <nvpair name="cmd_prompt" value="/admin1-&gt;" id="FenceSQ1-instance_attributes-cmd_prompt"/>
          <nvpair name="ipaddr" value="192.168.12.130" id="FenceSQ1-instance_attributes-ipaddr"/>
          <nvpair name="login" value="stoasadmin" id="FenceSQ1-instance_attributes-login"/>
          <nvpair name="passwd" value="pw4osstsvr00150800" id="FenceSQ1-instance_attributes-passwd"/>
          <nvpair name="pcmk_host_list" value="mysql1.moodle.hosting.local" id="FenceSQ1-instance_
          attributes-pcmk_host_list"/>
        </instance_attributes>
        <operations>
          <op name="monitor" interval="30s" id="FenceSQ1-monitor-30s"/>
        </operations>
        <meta_attributes id="FenceSQ1-meta_attributes">
          <nvpair name="target-role" value="Started" id="FenceSQ1-meta_attributes-target-role"/>
        </meta_attributes>
      </primitive>
    </resources>
    <constraints/>
  </configuration>
```

```
    <status>
      <node_state id="mysql2.moodle.hosting.local" uname="mysql2.moodle.hosting.local" in_ccm="true"
      crmd="online" crm-debug-origin="do_update_resource" join="member" expected="member">
        <transient_attributes id="mysql2.moodle.hosting.local">
          <instance_attributes id="status-mysql2.moodle.hosting.local">
            <nvpair id="status-mysql2.moodle.hosting.local-probe_complete" name="probe_complete"
            value="true"/>
          </instance_attributes>
        </transient_attributes>
        <lrm id="mysql2.moodle.hosting.local">
          <lrm_resources>
            <lrm_resource id="FenceSQ1" type="fence_drac5" class="stonith">
              <lrm_rsc_op id="FenceSQ1_last_0" operation_key="FenceSQ1_monitor_0" operation="monitor"
              crm-debug-origin="build_active_RAs" crm_feature_set="3.0.7" transition-
              key="4:0:7:a63f6998-a28f-47de-a5d4-556478e3fc71" transition-magic="0:7;4:0:7:a63f6998-
              a28f-47de-a5d4-556478e3fc71" call-id="5" rc-code="7" op-status="0" interval="0" last-
              run="1395412070" last-rc-change="1395412070" exec-time="1" queue-time="0" op-digest="70a
              09aaf1ff48a25e3db5aa620331d03"/>
            </lrm_resource>
</status>
</cib>
```

In the CIB, you can find two main parts. The first part contains the cluster configuration. The latter part contains status information. Within the configuration part of the cluster, there are three different main parts. First is the crm_config. This part contains generic configuration parameters that apply to the entire Pacemaker layer. Next is the <nodes> section. Here, you can find all nodes that are currently a part of the cluster. Last is the resources section. Here, all the resources that are managed by the cluster are defined.

The last part of the CIB is also the lengthiest part. It contains current status information about the resources in the cluster. This is important debugging information for cluster administrators, as it tells exactly what has been happening in the cluster recently. In Listing 4-2, you can see a schematic overview of the CIB composition.

Listing 4-2. CIB Schematic Overview

```
<configuration>
  <crm_config>
  ..
  </crm_config>
  <nodes>
  ..
  </nodes>
  <resources>
    <primitive>
    ..
    </primitive>
</configuration>
<status>
  ..
</status>
```

In the preceding CIB example, you see the different elements that make up the cluster. It all starts with the cluster generic settings, which specify general properties of the cluster. Then there is a definition of the nodes, which are the members of the cluster. Following that, there is the resource configuration, and in the end, there is an overview of the current status of the cluster.

As a cluster administrator, you will mostly deal with resource management. There are different types of resources, as follows:

- *Primitives*: A primitive is a service that is managed by the cluster. It's a single instance of the service, and it is comparable to services, as they are managed by sysctl, or runlevels, on a non-clustered node.

- *Groups*: A group is a collection of primitives. The advantage of working with groups is that the cluster will start the primitives that are part of the group, in the order that they are defined in the group. The cluster will also always keep the primitives in the same group together. If one primitive in a group fails, no subsequent primitives can be started.

- *Clones*: A clone is a primitive that needs to be started by the cluster more than once. Clones are useful for services that have to be started in an active/active mode, such as clustered file systems.

- *Master slaves*: A master slave is a special kind of clone, of which some instances (at least one) are the active master, and other instances are slave. Master slave resources are relatively rare. In Chapter 10, you will read how this resource type is used for the Distributed Replicated Block Device (DRBD).

crmd

The cluster resource manager daemon (crmd) is the process that manages the actual state of the cluster. The main task of the crmd is to direct the information flow between the various components of the cluster, such as resource placement on specific nodes. It also takes care of node transitions, where nodes go to another state.

On every cluster, there is a crmd process on each node. One of these is the master. The node where the master crmd is actually operational is recognized as the designated coordinator (DC). If the DC is on a node that fails, the cluster will automatically select a new DC quickly.

pengine

The Cluster Information Base (CIB) provides a declarative description of the desired cluster state, and the policy engine (pengine) is the part of the cluster that computes how it should be achieved. This generates a list of instructions that is sent to the crmd. The easiest way for an administrator to influence the behavior of the pengine is by defining constraints in the cluster. You can read more about constraint definitions in Chapter 8.

lrmd

The local resource manager daemon (lrmd) is a part of the cluster that runs on every cluster node as well. If the crmd decides that a particular resource should run on a specific node, it will instruct the lrmd on that node to start the resource. In case that doesn't work, the lrmd will get back to the crmd and disclose that starting the resource has failed. The cluster can then try to start the resource on another node in the cluster. The LRM also takes care of issuing monitor operations and stop operations on resources that are running on specific nodes.

stonithd/fenced

The stonithd process (or its equivalent, fenced, on Red Hat–based clusters) receives instructions from the crmd about changed node states. If a cluster node doesn't reply anymore on the cluster membership layer, the cluster membership layer will tell the crmd, and the crmd instructs stonithd to terminate that node. This is vital for proper operation of the cluster, and even if the software (still) allows administrators to define clusters without stonithd, you should never do that, because it makes for an unreliable cluster. In Chapter 5, you'll read how to configure base cluster settings as well as STONITH.

Cluster Management Tools

To modify the current state of the cluster, different management tools are available. In the end, they all do the same: modify the current state of the cluster as it is kept in the CIB.

Even if different management tools exist, in this book, I'll mainly demonstrate how the cluster is managed from the CRM shell. This tool provides an easy-to-use interface that works well from command-line environments and allows you to script cluster management tasks. If you prefer managing the cluster from a graphical environment, Hawk is the recommended solution. In this section, you will learn how to work with both. The other tools that are available are recommended for occasional use only. For that reason, I won't cover them in depth.

crm shell

The crm shell (see Listing 4-3) provides a direct interface to CIB. Newer versions of the crm shell also allow configuration of the Corosync layer and other parts of the cluster. You'll notice that new features are being added constantly. It is installed by default on some Linux distributions, but not on all. If you can type the crm command, you're good to go; if that doesn't work, make sure to install the crmsh package for your distribution.

Typing the crm command opens the crm shell interactive interface. Instead of opening the crm interface and working from there, you can also choose to type the complete command from the bash command line. You'll see some examples later in this subsection.

Listing 4-3. crm Shell Interface

```
node1:~ # crm
crm(live)# help

This is the CRM command line interface program.

Available commands:

        cib             manage shadow CIBs
        resource        resources management
        configure       CRM cluster configuration
        node            nodes management
        options         user preferences
        history         CRM cluster history
        site            Geo-cluster support
        ra              resource agents information center
        status          show cluster status
        quit,bye,exit   exit the program
        help            show help
        end,cd,up       go back one level

crm(live)#
```

From the crm shell interface, different commands are offered. Each of these has sub-commands as well. In order to choose the right option, it makes sense to know what these commands are all about. Table 4-1 provides an overview.

Table 4-1. *Explanation of Main* `crm` *Shell Features*

Command	Function
`cib`	Use this to work with shadow CIBs. These allow you to first apply all changes offline and, once you're satisfied with the modifications, apply them to the live cluster. Working with shadow CIBs is covered in Chapter 9 of this book.
`resource`	This is one of the most important commands. It allows you to manage the current status of resources in the cluster.
`configure`	This important command has options to configure resources and generic cluster properties. It also offers commands to make backups of the current cluster state or load a previous configuration from a text file.
`node`	This allows you to manage the current state of nodes, such as deleting nodes or setting nodes in maintenance mode.
`options`	This contains some commands that allow you to specify the environment from which the cluster administrator works.
`history`	Here, you'll find commands that help you browse cluster maintenance history.
`site`	This command category is used for environments in which a cluster between different sites has to be created.
`ra`	This command category provides all you need to manage and view resource agent scripts. It contains some useful commands that help you find out which properties are available for specific resource types.
`status`	This shows the cluster status, equivalent to using the `crm_mon` command.
`quit, bye, exit`	These close the `crm` shell.
`help`	This gives usage help.
`end, cd, up`	Use these commands to go back one level in the shell interface.

From the `crm` main shell interface, you can type any of the commands listed in Table 4-1, to enter a specific management environment.

Type, for example, `configure`, if you require access to specific cluster-management commands. This brings you to the interface that you can see in Listing 4-4.

Listing 4-4. From the Main Shell to the `configure` Subtree of the Configuration

```
crm(live)configure# help

This level enables all CIB object definition commands.
The configuration may be logically divided into four parts:
nodes, resources, constraints, and (cluster) properties and
attributes.  Each of these commands support one or more basic CIB
objects.

Nodes and attributes describing nodes are managed using the
`node` command.
```

Commands for resources are:

- `primitive`
- `monitor`
- `group`
- `clone`
- `ms`/`master` (master-slave)

In order to streamline large configurations, it is possible to define a template which can later be referenced in primitives:

- `rsc_template`

In that case the primitive inherits all attributes defined in the template.

There are three types of constraints:

- `location`
- `colocation`
- `order`

Finally, there are the cluster properties, resource meta attributes defaults, and operations defaults. All are just a set of attributes. These attributes are managed by the following commands:

- `property`
- `rsc_defaults`
- `op_defaults`

In addition to the cluster configuration, the Access Control Lists (ACL) can be setup to allow access to parts of the CIB for users other than `root` and `hacluster`. The following commands manage ACL:

- `user`
- `role`

The changes are applied to the current CIB only on ending the configuration session or using the `commit` command.

Comments start with `#` in the first line. The comments are tied to the element which follows. If the element moves, its comments will follow.

Available commands:

node	define a cluster node
primitive	define a resource
monitor	add monitor operation to a primitive
group	define a group
clone	define a clone

```
    ms                define a master-slave resource
    rsc_template      define a resource template
    location          a location preference
    colocation        colocate resources
    order             order resources
    rsc_ticket        resources ticket dependency
    property          set a cluster property
    rsc_defaults      set resource defaults
    role              define role access rights
    user              define user access rights
    op_defaults       set resource operations defaults
    show              display CIB objects
    edit              edit CIB objects
    filter            filter CIB objects
    delete            delete CIB objects
    default-timeouts  set timeouts for operations to minimums from the meta-data
    rename            rename a CIB object
    refresh           refresh from CIB
    erase             erase the CIB
    ptest             show cluster actions if changes were committed
    cib               CIB shadow management
    cibstatus         CIB status management and editing
    template          edit and import a configuration from a template
    commit            commit the changes to the CIB
    verify            verify the CIB with crm_verify
    upgrade           upgrade the CIB to version 1.0
    save              save the CIB to a file
    load              import the CIB from a file
    xml               raw xml
    quit              exit the program
    help              show help
    end               go back one level

crm(live)configure#
```

As you can see, in some of the sub-shells, many sub-commands are available, and detailed help about using the specific sub-environment is available as well. To get back from a sub-shell to the parent shell, you can type end. Another useful feature in the crm shell is tab completion. Just type the beginning of the command you want to use, and then press tab to complete the command.

Apart from moving to a specific location within the crm shell, you can also type on a bash command line everything you need. That means that you can choose either to type crm, then configure, and then edit, or you can just type the command crm configure edit from a bash shell environment. The latter approach works best when you're at ease with the options that are available, and it provides a great opportunity to use cluster-management commands in automated and scripted environments. Throughout the rest of this book, you'll find many examples of how to use the crm command to create a specific configuration.

Hawk

Hawk is the High Availability Web Konsole. Hawk has been made available for SUSE Linux Enterprise, OpenSUSE, Debian, and Fedora. You can, however, use the Fedora built on Red Hat and on similar distributions as well. Also, it's open source, so source code is available, and you're welcome to compile it. As all of the Hawk development occurs on the SUSE Linux Enterprise Server, the information in this section is based on the SLES configuration.

Hawk consists of two parts. First, there is the Hawk service script. You need to start it on the node that you want to use for enabling Hawk access. Once started, you can access the Hawk-management interface from a browser.

Before you can use Hawk, you must configure a user account. This user account has to be a member of the haclient group, and you have to provide a password for this user. You could use the hacluster or any other user you want to employ for cluster administration in Hawk. Make sure this user has a password, before you first start up the Hawk service. Then use `systemctl start hawk.service` to start the Hawk service (or `service hawk start`, if you're on a Linux that uses System V init for starting services). This runs the service on https port 7630 on that specific node.

To connect to Hawk, start a browser and enter the URL `https://yourserver:7630`. You'll see a message indicating that your connection with the server is untrusted (unless a trusted certificate has been installed). Proceed anyway, until you see the login prompt. On that prompt, enter the username hacluster (or the name of any other user that you have made a member of the haclient group) and provide the password. Next, click login to connect to the cluster. Figure 4-3 shows a cluster summary.

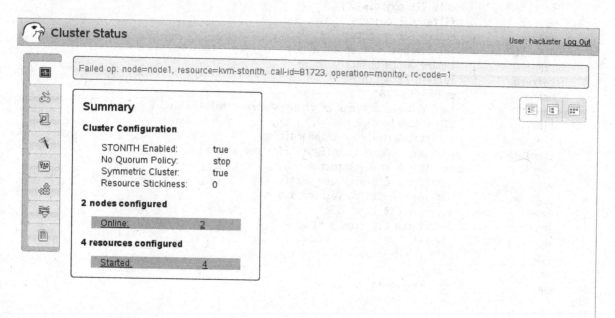

Figure 4-3. *Cluster summary in Hawk*

Hawk provides different views, which are available through three buttons at the upper-right of the hawk interface. To get insight on the current state of the cluster, you may prefer the tree view. This gives a hierarchical overview of all the resources that are currently configured in the cluster (Figure 4-4).

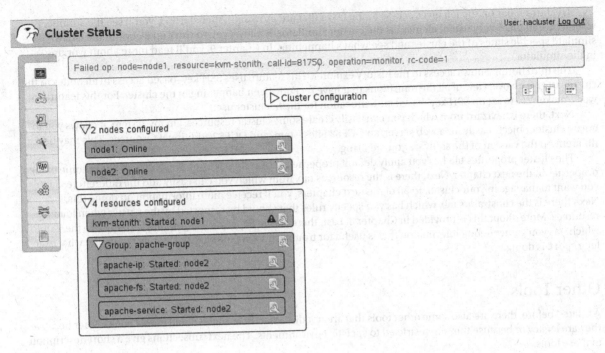

Figure 4-4. *Tree view*

To get an overview of which resources are started on which server, you may prefer the table view (Figure 4-5). This view is especially useful when troubleshooting the current state of larger clusters.

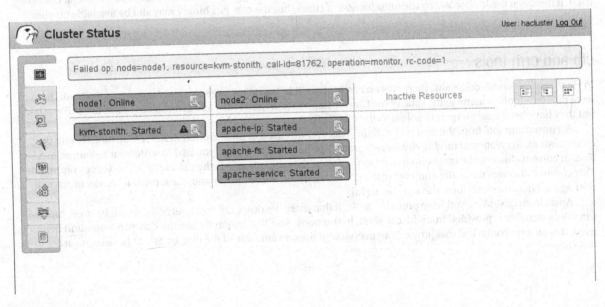

Figure 4-5. *Table view*

The button bar on the left gives access to the tasks that are provided. After starting, you'll see the summary screen by default. A very useful element is the cluster simulator. It allows you to work on a copy of the CIB to simulate specific states of the cluster and see what's happening. In Chapter 9, you'll read more about working in the simulator.

The third button allows access to the history explorer. This feature uses SSH key-based access to all nodes in the cluster, to give an overview of all the transitions that have recently been happening in the cluster. For this feature to work, make sure to set up SSH key-based authentication for the hacluster user.

Next, there is a wizard from which you can easily create some cluster resources. On my system, it allows you to create cluster objects easily for a web server, an OCFS2 Filesystem, and OCFS2 additional resources. This may be different on the version of the software you are using.

The cluster properties tab has you apply default properties to the entire cluster. You will read about some of these properties in the next chapter. Next, there is the resources tab, from which you can easily add the different resources you want to manage in your cluster. In all of the next chapters, you'll receive more information on doing this. Next, there is the constraints tab, which has you specify rules that should be respected by the cluster when loading resources. More about this is provided in Chapter 8. Last, there is run hb_report, a graphical interface to the Y utility, which has you gather debug information that is useful for troubleshooting the cluster. Chapter 9 tells you what exactly hb_report is doing.

Other Tools

As stated before, there are also some other tools that are not discussed in as much detail in this book, either because they are legacy or because they are restricted to specific environments. The next subsections give a short description of these tools.

crm_gui

In previous versions of Pacemaker, crm_gui (previously available as hb_gui) was the only graphical tool that could be used. It has been made obsolete by the introduction of Hawk, but the crm_gui binary may still be available on your distribution.

cib and crm tools

In Heartbeat version 2, originally, there was no easily accessible tool to manage cluster components. Instead, there were different tools to manage the state of the Cluster Information Base (CIB) and crmd. These tools are still available, but they have been made largely obsolete by the crm shell.

An important tool from the past is cibadmin. This tool was used to push chunks of XML code directly into the configuration, to create and modify cluster resources. Yes, back in those days, you had to write your resources in XML first. In current clusters, the most important manipulation that still remains is the cibadmin -E --force command. This command erases the entire contents of the CIB on all nodes in the cluster and, thus, provides a way to start all over again. On some occasions, this may be useful.

Apart from cibadmin, you have probably noticed that there are other crm tools. All of these can be used, but the same functionality is provided from the crm shell. In this book, you'll occasionally see the crm_mon command being used. It is an easy command that provides an overview of the current state of the cluster, as you have seen earlier in this chapter.

pcs

When Red Hat launched its Pacemaker stack on Red Hat 6, it created the pcmk (contained in the pcs package) command with it. This command aims to eventually provide functionality similar to that of the crm shell. As the Y shell currently is available in repositories for all distributions and pcs is not, I don't cover it in depth in this book. This is also because it isn't as feature-rich as crmsh. You will see some examples, however, in chapters where specific features for Red Hat clusters are discussed.

Conga: Luci and Ricci

Conga is the solution that provides the luci and ricci services. Luci and ricci are also specific to Red Hat environments. Ricci is an agent that has to be started on all nodes in the cluster. In a Pacemaker cluster, it interfaces to the crmd, to get status information and send changes to the cluster. The luci service has to be installed on a server that doesn't specifically have to be a cluster node. Luci contacts the different ricci nodes to interface with them. From Conga, you'll have a web interface that allows you to manage and monitor the cluster.

Summary

In this chapter, you have learned how Linux clusters are organized. You have read about architecture and how the cluster membership layer performs a role that is much different from the role of the cluster resource manager layer. In the next chapter, you will learn how to start building the lower layers of the cluster.

CHAPTER 5

■ ■ ■

Configuring Essential Cluster Settings

When setting up a cluster, there are some basic settings to take care of. These are settings that apply to the entire cluster and define how the cluster is operating under specific conditions. Also, you have to make sure that STONITH (Shoot The Other Node In The Head), also known as fencing, is taken care of. This chapter shows you how and introduces the following topics:

- Specifying default cluster settings
- Setting up STONITH
- Using fencing on Red Hat clusters

Specifying Default Cluster Settings

Before creating anything in the cluster, you should take a minute to think about some default cluster settings. By default, the cluster is designed to work well without changing any of the cluster properties. In specific situations, however, it does make sense to change the defaults for a few settings, as follows:

- `no-quorum-policy`
- `default-resource-stickiness`
- `stonith-action`

no-quorum-policy

The quorum is the majority in the cluster. To avoid an occurrence of split brain, the cluster will only react if it has a quorum. Imagine a five-node cluster in which, owing to a network failure, two groups are formed: a three-node group and a two-node group. In that situation, only the three-node group has a majority. Therefore, only the three-node group will be able to run resources in the cluster. This is a very important setting, because if the two-node group also ran resources, a risk of resource corruption would arise. For that reason, the default `no-quorum-policy` is set to `stop`.

The following `no-quorum-policy` settings are available:

- `stop`: This is the default setting. If quorum is lost, all resources are stopped immediately, to ensure that only a cluster that has a majority can run resources.
- `ignore`: This is what was needed in a two-node cluster using a Corosync version older than 2.3.x. A two-node cluster would always lose quorum if one node went down. To ensure that resources can still operate, set `no-quorum-policy` to `ignore`. In Corosync 2.3 and later, the quorum is provided by Corosync, which has a two-node setting. By giving this the value of 1, the quorum will automatically be handled the right way, even in a two-node cluster.

- `freeze`: If the quorum is lost, nothing will occur, and resources will just remain where they are. This might be needed, for example, where services such as OCFS2 and GFS2 can't stop cleanly in a partition that has become non-quorate. In such a situation, this is probably the sanest choice for everything. Services would be fenced if a quorate partition remained, but otherwise, it's the best shot at providing services.

- `suicide`: All nodes that themselves detect that they have lost quorum will self-fence.

The `no-quorum-policy` is set to the value `stop`, the default setting in clusters that consist of three or more nodes. It makes sense to use this in a three-node cluster, because in the event of split brain, where one node is running alone, it should really understand that it may never run any of the resources. That's exactly what the `no-quorum-policy stop` is doing: it stops all resources on a node that loses quorum, so that the other nodes in the cluster can safely take over the resources.

As discussed, in some cases, it makes sense to use `freeze` as the `no-quorum-policy` value. The procedure below describes how to do that.

1. Open a shell on one of the cluster nodes, either as root or as user hacluster.

2. Type `crm configure edit`. This brings you in a vim editing mode, in which you can change cluster parameters.

3. Locate the line that reads `property $id="cib-bootstrap-options"` and add the following line to the end: `no-quorum-policy="freeze"`.

4. Note the use of slashes. All lines that are not the last line in this part of the configuration should end with a slash (see the following listing).

```
property $id="cib-bootstrap-options" \
        dc-version="1.1.9-2db99f1" \
        cluster-infrastructure="classic openais (with plugin)" \
        expected-quorum-votes="2" \
        no-quorum-policy="ignore"
```

5. Write the changes and quit the editor interface. You have now successfully defined the required settings for a two-node cluster.

default-resource-stickiness

The `default-resource-stickiness` parameter can come in handy, if you want to influence where resources are placed. The default behavior is that resources will try to get back to the node that was originally servicing them. That means that after a failure, the resource will be moved over to another node in the cluster, and once the original node comes back, the resource will come back to the original node again. That is not ideal, as the user will experience a downtime twice. To prevent this from happening, you can set the `default-resource-stickiness` parameter.

This parameter takes a value between -1,000,000 and 1,000,000. (Don't use the commas when specifying these values. I have only included them here to increase readability!) A negative value means that the cluster will always remove it from its current location, which is pointless. So, don't use it, unless you want to demo a cluster with a lot of activity. The value of 0 normally means the resource will move back to its original location, and with a positive value, the resource will stay where it is. It is a good idea to use a moderate positive value here, such as 10,000, which means the cluster prefers leaving the resource where it is, preventing it from moving back to the original node with the downtime that is associated with that. You should realize, however, that it depends on the other weights that are used—for example, in the constraints. Do notice that resource stickiness can also be set on a per-resource basis.

stonith-action

As you can read in the next section of this chapter, STONITH is what stops a node at the moment cluster communication to the node fails. By default, after a STONITH (Shoot The Other Node In The Head) operation, the node will reboot and automatically be added to the cluster again. That might sound good, but if your node suffers from a serious problem, chances are that immediately after getting back in the cluster, it experiences the same problem and is restarted again. To prevent this from happening, you might want to add stonith-action="poweroff" to the cluster configuration. That ensures that after it has been killed by its peers, the node only comes back if it is manually restarted by the system administrator. Note that this can also be achieved by a setting for the SBD (STONITH Block Device) STONITH agent. Consult the man page for more details.

You can also configure the settings mentioned previously from the Hawk web interface. In Hawk, select the Cluster Properties tab on the left. Next, under Cluster Configuration, use the drop-down list to set all properties you want to configure for your cluster (Figure 5-1).

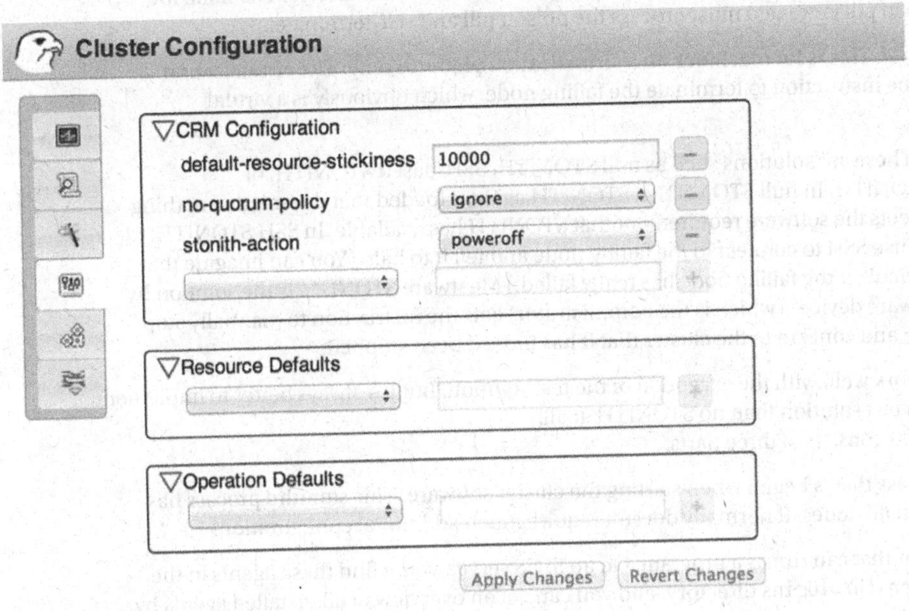

Figure 5-1. Setting cluster properties from Hawk

Setting Up STONITH

As discussed previously, STONITH (Shoot The Other Node In The Head) is a mandatory mechanism that guarantees the integrity of the cluster before moving over resources. Even if it is technically possible, you should never disable STONITH, as unpredictable results may occur. In some environments, STONITH is referred to as fencing. Both refer to the same mechanism. The acronym STONITH comes from Linux HA history, whereas in Red Hat HA clusters, the word *fencing* is more common.

Apart from the fact that STONITH guarantees integrity of resources in the cluster by terminating nodes that don't reply to the cluster anymore, it also is a requirement to move resources in the cluster. That means that when the cluster reacts on incidents, it won't move any resources until STONITH has confirmed that the failing node has been terminated. This is the essence of STONITH: it forces the failing node off the cluster and into a clean state, so that its resources can be started elsewhere. STONITH also helps in cleaning up transient/temporary errors and crashes.

Different Solutions

The essence of STONITH is that one of the cluster nodes that is still in a stable state and part of a quorate cluster has to send a message to a management mechanism for a failing node, so that it can be terminated. There's no need to bring it down in an orderly manner, just pulling the power plug is good enough. As you can imagine, a mechanism that is external to the operating system of the failing node is required for a good STONITH solution. Different approaches exist.

- *Hardware-based*: STONITH communicates to a hardware device, like a Dell DRAC (Dell Remote Access Controller), HP ILO, or IBM RSA management board that is integrated in the server. The management board gets the instruction to terminate the failing node. Another example of hardware-based STONITH is using a manageable power switch that can get the instruction from the cluster to terminate the failing node.

- *Based on shared disk*: The cluster writes a "poison pill" to a shared disk device. The node for which the poison pill is created must process the poison pill and self-terminate.

- *Hypervisor-based*: This is for machines on a virtualization platform only. The virtualization platform gets the instruction to terminate the failing node, which obviously is a virtual machine.

- *Test solutions*: These are solutions such as null STONITH, SSH-based STONITH, or "meatware" STONITH. In null STONITH, a STONITH agent is loaded that doesn't do anything at all. It only meets the software requirement that STONITH has available. In SSH STONITH, the cluster will use SSH to connect to the failing node and tell it to halt. (You can imagine that this may be difficult, if the failing node has really failed.) Meatware STONITH is the solution by which a "meatware device" (which is the administrator) gets the instruction to manually stop the failing node and confirm to the cluster that it has indeed been stopped.

All of these solutions work well, with the exception of the test solution. But it's always better to implement STONITH that is based on a test solution than no STONITH at all!

Every STONITH solution consists of three parts.

- A stonithd process that is begun when starting the cluster software. This stonithd process has to be running on all nodes. It normally doesn't require much additional configuration.

- A resource agent that can run as a program. On an SLES server, you'll find these agents in the /usr/lib64/stonith/plugins directory, and you can get an overview of all installed agents by using the stonith -L command.

- Instructions in the cluster that tell the cluster how to execute STONITH operations.

The generic approach for setting up STONITH is first to find out exactly how a specific STONITH agent should be used. A KVM-based STONITH agent, for example, requires a completely different approach than an IPMI (intelligent platform management interface)-based STONITH agent. In the procedural descriptions provided in the subsequent sections, you'll find specific instructions for some of the resource agents.

If you know how the STONITH agent works, you'll next have to run the agent without the cluster, to verify that you can operate STONITH actions from the command line. Once you've verified that, you can integrate the STONITH configuration in the cluster.

To use STONITH, you need a STONITH agent that supports the mechanism you want to use for STONITH. By default, many STONITH agents are installed. You may request a list of all of these by using the command stonith -l. Listing 5-1 shows what the output of this command looks like.

Listing 5-1. Using stonith -l to Get a List of Available STONITH Agents

```
node1:~ # stonith -L
apcmaster
apcmastersnmp
apcsmart
baytech
bladehpi
cyclades
drac3
external/drac5
external/dracmc-telnet
external/hetzner
external/hmchttp
external/ibmrsa
external/ibmrsa-telnet
external/ipmi
external/ippower9258
external/kdumpcheck
external/libvirt
external/nut
external/rackpdu
external/riloe
external/sbd
external/vcenter
external/vmware
external/xen0
external/xen0-ha
ibmhmc
ipmilan
meatware
nw_rpc100s
rcd_serial
rps10
suicide
wti_mpc
wti_nps
```

Setting Up libvirt Hypervisor-Based STONITH

As a hypervisor-based STONITH solution is relatively easy to set up, I'll discuss this setup in detail. In this section, you'll learn generic techniques that also apply to hardware and shared disk–based STONITH.

In this section, you'll also read how to set up STONITH for KVM virtual machines. This is a typical scenario that will be used in test environments in which multiple virtual machines are running on top of the same KVM hypervisor. The STONITH agent that manages virtual machines in a KVM environment talks to the libvirt daemon. libvirt is a process that can be used to manage virtual machines on either the KVM or the Xen virtualization platform.

1. The first step in the configuration of every STONITH agent is that you must set up access for the STONITH agent to the device. If the device is an ILO board in an HP server, you need a username and password. In this case, the STONITH "device" is a KVM hypervisor, so you need a means of allowing the STONITH agent to communicate with the KVM hypervisor. For this specific STONITH agent, SSH keys are the most efficient solution. The following steps help you set up SSH key–based authentication.

   a. Make sure that hostname resolving is set up properly, so that all cluster nodes and the KVM host can find one another based on their names.

   b. As root on the first cluster node, use `ssh-keygen -t dsa`. Press Enter to accept the default answers for all questions.

   c. Still on the first cluster node, use `ssh-copy-id ~/.ssh/id_dsa.pub kvmhost` to copy the SSH public key to the kvmhost. Replace "kvmhost" with the actual name of the KVM host.

   d. Repeat these commands on all other cluster nodes.

2. The libvirt STONITH agent that you are going to use to send STONITH commands to KVM virtual machines requires that the libvirt package be installed on all virtual machines. Use `zypper in libvirt` on all KVM virtual machines in the cluster now, to accomplish this. Without this package, the hypervisor won't be able to contact virtual machines in order to terminate them.

3. At this point, you should have met all prerequisites, and it's time for the first test. To start with, you should now request the parameters this STONITH agent requires. To do this, use `stonith -t external/libvirt -n`. The command shows you that the STONITH agent needs a hostlist, a hypervisor_uri, and a reboot_method. To use all these in the appropriate command, you can now run the following command:

```
stonith -t external/libvirt hostlist="node1,node2" hypervisor_uri="qemu+ssh://lin/system"
-T reset node1
```

In this command, numerous arguments are used. First, following -t, the name of the STONITH agent is referred to. This name must be the same as something you've seen in the output of the `stonith -L` command. Next, the `hostlist` parameter is used to give a comma-separated list of nodes that can be managed by this STONITH agent. Next, there is the `hypervisor_uri`. The URI starts with the access mechanism, which, in this case, is qemu+ssh (which means you're sending a command to the qemu layer using SSH). Next in the URI is the name of the KVM host, followed by `/system`. Following that is the STONITH action, which is defined with the option `-T reset` and is the last parameter you have of the name of the node to be STONITHed.

If the manual STONITH worked, you're ready to proceed. If it did not, you should check naming, which is the most common error for this STONITH agent. The names of the hosts you are addressing have to be recognized by the KVM hypervisor (run `virsh list` on the hypervisor to find out), and they also have to be the kernel names, as used on the nodes (use `uname -n` to find out). If the virsh list name doesn't match the uname -n name, this STONITH method isn't going to work, so make sure you fix it before going on!

At this point, you're ready to put all the required parameters in the cluster. You can, of course, take the easy approach and use the Hawk web interface, from which you can select all available options from the drop-down list. You can also add the resource directly into the cluster, using the crm shell interface. To be able to add the resource from the shell, you have to find out which parameters are supported by the resource you want to add. These are the parameters you've previously found with the `stonith -t external/libvirt -n` command. Next, the only thing you have to do is put them in the cluster, using the right syntax. The following procedure describes how to do this.

1. On one of the cluster nodes, as root or any user that has been granted CIB access, enter the command `crm`. This takes you into the `crm` shell.

2. Type `configure`. You are now in the configuration environment. Type `help` to see a list of all commands that are available. Now type `edit` to open the cluster editor. At this point, you should see something similar to Listing 5-2.

    Listing 5-2. Editing the Cluster Configuration

    ```
    node node1
    node node2
    property $id="cib-bootstrap-options" \
            dc-version="1.1.9-2db99f1" \
            cluster-infrastructure="classic openais (with plugin)" \
            expected-quorum-votes="2"
    #vim:set syntax=pcmk
    ~
    ~
    ~
    ~
    ~
    ~
    ~
    ~
    ~
    ~
    ~
    ~
    ~
    ~
    ~
    "/tmp/tmpFYbDVV.pcmk" 7L, 197C
    ```

3. As you are in a vim interface, you can use your normal editor skills to add the following block somewhere in the configuration:

    ```
    primitive stonith-libvirt stonith:external/libvirt \
            params hostlist="node1,node2" \
            hypervisor_uri="qemu+ssh://lin/system" \
            op monitor interval="60" timeout="20" \
            meta target-role="Started"
    ```

4. Now, type `commit`, to write the changes to the cluster, and type `exit`, to quit the `crm` shell. You can now verify that the STONITH agent is running somewhere in the cluster, using `crm_mon` or `crm status`.

    ```
    node2:~ # crm status
    ============
    Last updated: Tue Apr  1 03:40:30 2014
    Last change: Sat Mar 22 10:18:29 2014 by hacluster via crmd on node1
    Stack: openais
    ```

57

```
Current DC: node1 - partition with quorum
Version: 1.1.6-b988976485d15cb702c9307df55512d323831a5e
2 Nodes configured, 2 expected votes
1 Resources configured.
============

Online: [ node1 node2 ]

 kvm-stonith          (stonith:external/libvirt):          Started node1
```

5. After configuring STONITH, you can run a STONITH test on either of the nodes, for instance, by using `killall -9 corosync`. That should put the node in an unreachable state and issue a STONITH action on the node.

Setting Up Hardware-Based STONITH: The APC Master Power Switch

As a cluster administrator, it is important that you be able to deal with STONITH in different environments. So, let's have a look at hardware-based STONITH and configure an APC Master power switch. This is a manageable multiple socket that servers are connected to to get their power. On an APC power switch, every socket has a port name, and as an administrator, you can configure which port contains which server. That means that from the cluster, you can tell the power switch to switch off power on a specific port, to switch off the node that is connected to that port. Note that hardware solutions such as the APC power switch have become more uncommon, because most servers nowadays come with management boards.

Before using the APC Master in your cluster, you have to set it up. You can use the following procedure to give the device an IP address. Before you start, make sure that the APC is connected to your LAN and that you have some servers connected to the power outlets of the APC.

1. Write down the MAC address of the device. You can find this address on a sticker on the device.

2. Use ARP to define an IP address for the device on your local computer. You won't really set the IP address on the device, but you will tell your computer that the device can be reached at this IP address—and that works fine for the further configuration. On Linux, you would do that using the following command:

   ```
   arp -s 192.168.1.245 00:c0:b7:4b:c9:d9
   ```

3. Now, use ping with a package size of 113 bytes to set the IP address on the local device as well.

   ```
   ping 192.168.1.245 -s 113
   ```

You will see the device answering to the ping package.

4. Use telnet to connect to the device. The default username is apc; the default password is also apc. Make sure to change the password, to prevent others from having fun with your equipment.

5. After logging in to the device, choose Network from the Console menu; select TCP/IP and then Manual boot mode. You need this to tell the device that it's not booting through a DHCP server.

6. Back in the main Network menu, specify the System IP, Subnet Mask, and Default Gateway address.

7. Use Ctrl+C to exit the Control Console menu, followed by option 4 to log out. This will write the changes to the device and make them persistent.

At this point, your APC device is ready for use in the cluster. Time for a small test. The following procedure outlines how you can power cycle a port on the APC.

1. Open a telnet session to the APC and enter the username and password that you've provided for the device (default for both is apc). This gives you the main menu, which you can see in Listing 5-3.

Listing 5-3. The Main Menu from Which You Can Control Access to the APC PDU

```
American Power Conversion          Network Management Card AOS      v3.7.0

(c) Copyright 2008 All Rights Reserved  Rack PDU APP             v3.7.0

-------------------------------------------------------------------------

Name      : RackPDU                     Date : 09/19/2000

Contact   : Unknown                     Time : 12:20:01

Location  : Unknown                     User : Administrator

Up Time   : 0 Days 0 Hours 5 Minutes    Stat : P+ N+ A+



Switched Rack PDU: Communication Established

:------- Control Console ------------------------------------------------

    1- Device Manager

    2- Network

    3- System

    4- Logout


    <ESC>- Main Menu, <ENTER>- Refresh, <CTRL-L>- Event Log
```

2. From the menu, select 1, to gain access to the device manager. This gives you access to three different options, from which you select option 2, Outlet Management.

3. At this point, select option 1, Outlet Control/Configuration. This gives you a list of all available power outlets and their current status. (See Listing 5-4)

Listing 5-4. The Outlet Control/Configuration Menu

```
------- Outlet Control/Configuration -------------------------------------

        1- Outlet 1                ON

        2- Outlet 2                ON

        3- Outlet 3                ON

        4- Outlet 4                ON

        5- Outlet 5                ON

        6- Outlet 6                ON

        7- Outlet 7                ON

        8- Outlet 8                ON

        9- Master Control/Configuration


        <ESC>- Back, <ENTER>- Refresh, <CTRL-L>- Event Log      >
```

4. Now, select the outlet that you want to shut down and say that you want to work on outlet 1. Next, choose option 1, Control Outlet.

5. At this point, you see the menu with available options (see Listing 5-5). From this menu, select Immediate Reboot and confirm your choice by typing "Yes." The power will now be recycled, and your server will reboot.

Listing 5-5. The Control Outlet Menu Gives You Different Power Management Options

```
------- Control Outlet ---------------------------------------------------

        Name      : Outlet 1

        Outlet    : 1

        State     : ON

    1- Immediate On

    2- Immediate Off

    3- Immediate Reboot

    4- Delayed On
```

5- Delayed Off

6- Delayed Reboot

7- Cancel

Now that you have a generic feeling for what you can do from the APC PDU, it's time to make it usable for your cluster. First, you have to think about how you want the nodes to be connected to the PDU's. You should make sure not to connect all nodes to one single PDU. That would make that PDU a single point of failure. So, if you are building a four-node cluster, connect two nodes to PDU1 and two nodes to PDU2, in which case your resources will survive a situation in which a PDU goes down. If your server has more than one power supply (which is quite common), make sure that they are all connected to the same PDU, or else it won't work.

Next, you have to set up the PDU itself. That means that you must configure a name for each of the ports of the device. The cluster is going to talk to the APC and tell it to switch down node1, for example. But in order to enable this, the APC has to know what it's talking to when talking to node1. Configure this by giving a name to each of the ports on the device. After doing that, you also have to set it up to use the Simple Network Management Protocol (SNMP). STONITH is going to use this protocol to talk to the device, and to configure this, you have to set a password that allows SNMP to make changes to the current configuration. The next procedure describes how to perform these two steps.

1. Open a telnet session to the PDU and log in with the username and password that are set on the device (defaults are apc, apc).

2. From the main menu, select option 1, Device Manager. Next, choose option 2, Outlet Management, followed by option 1, Outlet Control/Configuration. This allows access to the outlet configuration menu, from which you can enter a name for each of the outlets (Listing 5-6). Make sure that the name corresponds to the real hostname of the node.

Listing 5-6. The Outlet Control/Configuration Menu

```
------- Outlet Management --------------------------------------------------

    1- Outlet Control/Configuration

    2- Outlet Restriction

    <ESC>- Back, <ENTER>- Refresh, <CTRL-L>- Event Log

> 1

------- Outlet Control/Configuration ---------------------------------------

    1- node1              ON

    2- node2              ON

    3- SAN                ON

    4- Outlet 4           ON

    5- Outlet 5           ON

    6- Outlet 6           ON
```

```
 7- Outlet 7                    ON

 8- Outlet 8                    ON

 9- Master Control/Configuration

 <ESC>- Back, <ENTER>- Refresh, <CTRL-L>- Event Log
```

3. After configuring a name for the outlet, make sure that you select option 5, Accept Changes, to actually write the changes to the device. After doing that, press the Escape key five times, which brings you back to the main menu.

4. From the main menu, select Network, and from the Network menu, select SNMP. In the SNMP menu, select 2—SNMPv1 Specific Settings. This allows access to a list of four different access controls. Access control number 1 allows you to set the SNMP read community name; access control number 2 allows you to set the write community name. At this point, select option 2, which gives access to the default settings for the write community. It's a good idea to change to something more secure the default setting on which the community name *private* is used. (Otherwise, anyone who uses *private* as the community name to access your PDU will have complete write access to the device!)

5. After making the changes, select option 4, to accept the changes and write them to the device. Next, press Escape until you get back to the main menu, then log out from the device (Listing 5-7).

Listing 5-7. Change the Default Write Community Name *private* to Something That Is More Secure

```
------- SNMPv1 Access Control 2 -------------------------------------------------

     Access Control Summary

     #  Community       Access        NMS IP

     -----------------------------------------------------------------------

     1  public          Read          0.0.0.0

     2  private         Write         0.0.0.0

     3  public2         Disabled      0.0.0.0

     4  private2        Disabled      0.0.0.0

 1- Community Name: private

 2- Access Type   : Write

 3- NMS IP/Name   : 0.0.0.0

 4- Accept Changes:

 ?- Help, <ESC>- Back, <ENTER>- Refresh, <CTRL-L>- Event Log
```

You have now used manual power cycling on a host, and you have set up the PDU to communicate to the cluster. Following the next procedure, you'll learn how to set up the cluster to use the PDU for STONITH operations.

1. Make sure Hawk is started on one of the cluster nodes and log in to it.

2. Click Resources and add a Resource ID. Choose, for example, the Resource ID apc-stonith and select the class stonith.

3. Note that there are different resource agents that seem to make sense. To control a power switch using the SNMP protocol, select the type external/rackpdu.

4. Make sure all of the required parameters have the appropriate values. You must at least specify the following three parameters:

   - community: This is the SNMP community name that is needed to connect to the power switch.

   - hostlist: Set this to AUTO, to query the device for all hostnames that are available, or specify the names of the cluster nodes manually.

   - pduip: This is the IP address of the device.

5. Now, you can set the target-role to Started and create the resource.

You should now have a working resource for the APC master device. Listing 5-8 shows what its configuration looks like from the crm shell.

Listing 5-8. APC Master STONITH Device Configuration

```
primitive apc-stonith stonith:external/rackpdu \
        params pduip="192.168.122.22" hostlist="AUTO" community="private" \
        op start interval="0" timeout="20" \
        op stop interval="0" timeout="15" \
        op monitor interval="3600" timeout="20" start-delay="15" \
        meta target-role="Started"
```

Configuring STONITH for Dell DRAC and Other Server Management Cards, Such As HP ILO

Many server brands are equipped with a management card. This management card has its own operating system, and it allows you to manage the state of the server. As an administrator, you can log in to the management card and manually restart a server, for example. In a cluster, you can create a resource agent to do this automatically for you.

There is a challenge when working with DRAC hardware, which is that there are so many versions of it. The DRAC (Dell Remote Access Controller) version that is supported quite well in the cluster is DRAC5. From DRAC6 on, you have to enter a bit of additional configuration.

Before setting up the STONITH resource agent in the cluster, you have to make sure that you can connect to it from the cluster. This involves a number of tasks.

1. Configure the DRAC device on its own network and make sure that the DRAC network interfaces can be reached from the console of the cluster nodes. If you cannot ping the DRAC interfaces, you certainly won't be able to log in and perform STONITH operations.

2. Set the DRAC username and password. You'll need these to connect to it from the STONITH RA.

3. Enable SSH.

After configuring the DRAC BIOS, boot the server. Once it is up and running again (and you have performed this procedure on all the nodes in your cluster), you can start configuring the resource.

The basic resource agent to use to configure DRAC is the DRAC5 resource agent. It is the starting point for all DRAC management cards. Alternatively, you can use the IPMI resource agent. This agent uses IPMI, a generic set of commands that can be used on different resource agents.

The DRAC5 resource agent is using a relatively simple shell script: /usr/lib64/stonith/plugins/external/ drac5. The foundation of this script is that it is using SSH to log in to the DRAC card and execute a command. To execute the command, the racadm command is used, followed by the action that has to be performed. The following line contains the foundation of all that the DRAC5 resource agent is doing:

```
/usr/bin/ssh -q -x -n $userid$ipaddr racadm serveraction "$1"
```

The specific command that is passed to the DRAC interface is specified as the first argument of the script. For instance, if the reset argument is used, the racadm command hardreset is used to reset the server.

What makes dealing with the default resource agent a bit tough is that it knows only three default parameters: hostname, ipaddr, and userid. The hostname is the name of the host that needs to be managed; the ipaddr refers to the IP address of the DRAC card; and userid is the ID of the user who needs to log in to the device. That means that the resource agent has to be started with the right argument to start with. Even if the script has different arguments that can be used (such as gethosts, on, off, reset, and more), the CRM has no option to pick from these different arguments. That is why the default-stonith-action parameter is used instead. The second thing that makes using this agent a bit difficult is that you cannot specify a password to log in with. Instead, the DRAC device has to be configured for SSH-based login.

The configuration of the resource for the DRAC STONITH agent can resemble Listing 5-9.

Listing 5-9. DRAC Device Configuration

```
primitive drac-node1 stonith:external/drac5 \
        params ipaddr="192.168.10.1" hostname="node1" userid="dracadmin" \
        op start interval="0" timeout="20" \
        op stop interval="0" timeout="15" \
        op monitor interval="3600" timeout="20" start-delay="15" \
        meta target-role="Started"
```

Because the DRAC STONITH agent is relatively small, and because it does make sense to understand how a fencing agent can be organized, Listing 5-10 gives the content of the resource agent on an SLES 11 SP3 server. It is recommended to have a look at it, even if you don't use DRAC, because understanding how resource agents are organized is really helpful for troubleshooting them.

Listing 5-10. Contents of the DRAC5 Resource Agent

```
node1:/usr/lib64/stonith/plugins/external # vim drac5
#!/bin/sh
#
# External STONITH module for DRAC5 adapters.
#
# Author:  Jun Wang
# License:     GNU General Public License (GPL)
#
...
```

```
drac_on() {
        sshlogin poweron
}

drac_off() {
        sshlogin poweroff
}

drac_status() {
        sshlogin powerstatus
}

case $1 in
gethosts)
        echo $hostname
        ;;
on)
        drac_poweron
        ;;
off)
        drac_poweroff
        ;;
reset)
        drac_reset
        ;;
status)
        drac_status
        ;;
getconfignames)
        for i in hostname ipaddr userid; do
                echo $i
        done
        ;;
getinfo-devid)
        echo "DRAC5 STONITH device"
        ;;
getinfo-devname)
        echo "DRAC5 STONITH device"
        ;;
getinfo-devdescr)
        echo "DRAC5 host reset/poweron/poweroff"
        ;;
getinfo-devurl)
        echo "http://www.dell.com"
        ;;
getinfo-xml)
        cat <<EOF
<parameters>
```

```
<parameter name="hostname" unique="1">
<content type="string" />
<shortdesc lang="en">
Hostname
</shortdesc>
<longdesc lang="en">
The hostname of the host to be managed by this STONITH device
</longdesc>
</parameter>

<parameter name="ipaddr" unique="1">
<content type="string" />
<shortdesc lang="en">
IP Address
</shortdesc>
<longdesc lang="en">
The IP address of the STONITH device
</longdesc>
</parameter>

<parameter name="userid" unique="1">
<content type="string" />
<shortdesc lang="en">
Login
</shortdesc>
<longdesc lang="en">
The username used for logging in to the STONITH device
</longdesc>
</parameter>

</parameters>
EOF
        ;;
*)
        exit 1
        ;;
esac
```

IPMI and Other Management Boards

Because there is no standard for server management cards, a generic solution was created to interface with them. This is IPMI. Many vendors, including Dell, HP, and IBM provide support for the IPMI standard. That means that instead of passing vendor-specific commands to the management card, you can use IPMI commands, which are supposed to work on all management cards. Before using them, you should, however, always make sure that IPMI support is enabled on the management cards that you're using!

The IPMI resource agent uses the `ipmitool` command. This is a binary that should be installed on your server and which you can use to send specific commands to an IPMI-enabled interface. Use the command `ipmitool --help` to find out which arguments can be used with it. To use it in an automated way from the IPMI management interface, you can use the following parameters in the IPMI STONITH resource:

- `hostname`: The name of the host that should be STONITHed
- `interface`: The IPMI interface, typically set to LAN
- `ipaddr`: The IP address of the IPMI device
- `ipmitool`: If not in the `$PATH`, this should be the complete path of the `ipmitool` command.
- `passwd`: The password used to log in to the device
- `userid`: The username needed to log in to the IPMI device

Setting Up Shared Disk-Based STONITH

A convenient method for setting up STONITH is to use the STONITH Block Device (SBD). This STONITH method needs access to a shared disk device, so you can only use it if an SAN disk is available. On the SAN disk, you have to create a small partition (8MB is enough) to store the SBD STONITH information. For reliability, three devices can be used instead of one, if possible.

SBD STONITH is based on the principle of a poison pill. If a node has to be terminated, a poison pill is written for that node in the SBD partition. Eating the poison pill is mandatory, which means that as long as the SBD process on the failing node is still available, it will process the poison pill and commit suicide.

In the following procedure, you'll learn how to set up an SBD-based STONITH.

1. Make sure a shared device is available and create a small, 8MB partition on the device. Do NOT put a file system on the partition; an unformatted partition is enough!

2. From one of the nodes connected to the shared device, you have to initialize the shared device. To do this, use `sbd -d /dev/sdc1 create`. (Read carefully, the command is sbd, not SBD!) Also, you should consider using `/dev/disk/by-id` names, which won't change, instead of short names like `/dev/sdc1`.

3. Verify that the SBD metadata are written to the device, using `sbd -d /dev/sdc1 dump`. This should show something similar to Listing 5-11.

Listing 5-11. Verifying SBD Metadata

```
node2:~ # sbd -d /dev/sdc1 dump
==Dumping header on disk /dev/sdc1
Header version     : 2.1
UUID               : aaa1b226-8c0c-45ac-9f88-8fe5571f8fc7
Number of slots    : 255
Sector size        : 512
Timeout (watchdog) : 5
Timeout (allocate) : 2
Timeout (loop)     : 1
Timeout (msgwait)  : 10
==Header on disk /dev/sdc1 is dumped
```

4. To protect your configuration from a system hang (where stonithd can no longer be addressed to crash the failing node), it is mandatory to load a watchdog module in the kernel. Some hardware has a specific watchdog, if your hardware doesn't, you can load the software-based watchdog softdog. To make sure that this module is loaded upon a system start, open /etc/init.d/boot.local with an editor and put the line modprobe softdog in this file. You should, however, use softdog only as a last resort. A hardware-assisted watchdog is the only reliable protection against the kernel crashing.

5. To use SBD STONITH, you also have to make sure the sbd daemon is started with the cluster. On systemd-based systems, this is done via the sbd.service file (which automatically groups itself with Pacemaker). Up to SLES 11, this process was started from the openais cluster load script, but it needs a configuration file /etc/sysconfig/sbd that has the following contents:

```
SBD_DEVICE="/dev/sdc1"
SBD_OPTS="-W -P"
```

Note that making an error here has severe consequences: if the SBD device is not available, the cluster will not start. At this point, it's a good idea to restart the nodes in the cluster.

6. After restart, you can use the sbd -d /dev/sdc1 list command. This gives an overview of nodes that have the sbd daemon started and are currently using the SBD STONITH device.

```
node1:~ # sbd -d /dev/sdc1 list
0        node2        clear
1        node1        clear
```

7. Now, it's time for a first test. Use the following command to effectuate a STONITH operation from the command line: stonith -t external/sbd sbd_device=/dev/sdc1 -T reset node2. This should crash the node.

8. If the preceding test worked well, you can perform a second test and see if the watchdog is doing its work. On one of the nodes, use echo c > /proc/sysrq-trigger to crash the node. If the watchdog is doing its work properly, the node will be STONITHed.

9. If your previous tests have all succeeded, you can now add the resource agent to the cluster. Use crm configure edit and add the following line to the cluster configuration:

```
primitive sbd-stonith stonith:external/sbd \
```

10. You can now use crm_mon to verify the current cluster configuration and check that the STONITH agent has properly loaded.

Using Fencing on Red Hat Clusters

If you understand how to use STONITH, you'll also understand how to use fencing. On Red Hat clusters, the fence daemon fenced is used with its own specific resource agent scripts to implement the same functionality as STONITH. All of the basic building blocks are the same as in STONITH; only the resource scripts are different. (If you require fencing and not STONITH, it's still a good idea to read the section about STONITH, to get a general sense of how it works.)

A number of fence scripts are available on Red Hat systems, and you can run all of them as commands on the command line, as well as from the cluster, to pass the fencing parameters to the cluster automatically.

Because in some cases it requires some additional configuration on your fencing hardware, it is a good idea to test your fencing mechanism, using the fence commands from the command line before putting the configuration in the cluster. Have a look at the available command arguments before trying them, because they will be different on each fencing device. Once you've found out how a specific device is to be used, you can try a fencing operation from the command line. The following command, for example, would use fence_drac5 to send a fencing operation to node1 using SSH:

```
fence -a 192.168.100.1 -l dracadmin -p password -x
```

Continue only if you have confirmed that this command is exhibiting the expected behavior.

Before putting the configuration in the cluster, you should find out which are the available parameters. You can do this by using the crm ra meta command, which provides a large amount of detailed information. For example, use crm ra meta stonith:fence_drac5 to get an overview of all of the available parameters for DRAC5, including a description of how to use these parameters.

After finding out which parameters to use, you can include the fence device in the cluster configuration. In Listing 5-12, you can see what the configuration would look like to fence a specific node using the fence_drac5 agent.

Listing 5-12. Sample Fence Configuration for DRAC

```
primitive Fenceapache1 stonith:fence_drac5 \
        params action="reboot" cmd_prompt="/admin1->" ipaddr="192.168.12.97" login="admin"
passwd="secret" secure="1" pcmk_host_list="apache1.moodle.hosting.local" \
        op monitor interval="30s" \
        meta target-role="Started"
```

Summary

In this chapter, you have read how to build the basic cluster configuration. You have learned how to set some basic cluster parameters and how to work with STONITH or fencing to guarantee the integrity of resources in the cluster. In the next chapter, you'll discover how to add services to the cluster to be managed as cluster resources.

■ ■ ■

## CHAPTER 6

Clustering Resources

At this point, all the prerequisites are met, and it's time to start creating some cluster resources. In this chapter, you'll read how to create a basic configuration; in later chapters, you'll learn how to work with more advanced parameters.

What Makes Clustered Resources Different

The purpose of high availability is to make sure your vital resources will be available at all times. To accomplish that goal, you have to make sure that the resources are not started by the node's init system but that they are managed by the cluster. That means that you must take the resources out of the systemd enabled services, so that the cluster is the only software taking care of starting them.

There are many ways to start resources. A simple cluster can start a service without any further dependencies. But you'll have to deal with dependency requirements soon enough. It's like starting resources on a local machine, with which, for instance, you have to take care that the file systems are loaded before the services that use these file systems. On clusters, that's not much different. In the next sections, we'll work out the case of clustering an Apache file server.

Clustering an Apache File Server

In this first example, you'll learn how to cluster a typical Apache web service. The approach discussed here doesn't just work for an Apache web service; it's applicable to other services as well. So, even if you don't need Apache but something else—like a database, for instance—read this chapter, to learn how to set up resources in a clustered environment.

Understanding Resource Agents

To configure Apache in a cluster, you have to make sure that the Apache service can be reached, no matter where it is running. That means that it is not enough just to cluster the Apache web service, because no matter where it runs, the web service has to be accessible by the same IP address, and it must be able to access the same files in its document root. Typically, that means that you'll have to create three resources: an IP address, a file system, and a web service. Next, you must configure a group that is going to keep all these resources together, no matter where in the cluster they are activated.

To create resources, you need resource agents (RAs). A resource agent is like a service load script, as they were used in System-V runlevels, but a service script that contains cluster parameters as well. The resource agents are installed with the cluster, and they are subdivided into different classes.

- lsb: LSB (Linux Standard Base) resource agents are system V init scripts that can be started from the cluster. These scripts are not installed with the cluster but are installed with the operating system itself. When browsing these, you'll see only a list of all the scripts in the /etc/init.d directory. They don't contain any cluster information and should, therefore, only be used if no real cluster resource agents are available. Note that on a modern server that uses systemd, you won't see many LSB services.

- ocf: OCF (Open Cluster Framework) resource agents look a lot like LSB scripts, but they have specific parameters that relate to the cluster. They also often contain properties that normally are stored in configuration files. By storing these properties in the resource agent's configuration, they are easily made available on the node that has to run the resource agent. If you can choose between an OCF and an LSB resource agent, you should always use the OCF resource agent. OCF scripts come from different sources, and, therefore, you will find that there is a subdivision of the OCF RAs by their "provider."

  - heartbeat: These are the resource agents provided by the main resource-agents package. (The name of this provider has historical connotations, as the agents were originally packed with the Heartbeat project.)

  - linbit: These are RAs that are used for setting up a Distributed Replicated Block Device (DRBD) and related configuration. Read Chapter 9 for an example using DRBD.

  - lvm2: Some RAs that are needed for setting up clustered LVM logical volumes

  - OCFS2: Some RAs that are needed for setting up OCFS2 cluster shared file systems. See Chapter 7 for further details.

  - pacemaker: This contains the resource agents that are shipped with the Pacemaker project.

  - Other "provider" names are possible, as third parties may ship their own agents with their software.

- service: These resource agents are used to manage systemd service scripts from the cluster. As with LSB scripts, you better avoid using them, if an OCF alternative exists.

- stonith: These are the agents for STONITH, as previously discussed. While they are configured as primitives, they are not resource agents. They use completely different application programming interfaces (APIs) and have a different purpose.

Creating Resources

When adding resources to the cluster, it may be challenging to use the correct parameters. In the procedure following, you will learn how to discover parameters from the crm shell and how to add resources to the cluster, based on the parameters you've found. After creating the individual resources, you'll next learn how they can be joined together in a group. Before proceeding, make sure that Apache is installed and a file system is created on the shared storage device.

■ **Note** Before clustering anything, make sure the software is available to all nodes in the cluster. You could take care of this by setting up a shared file system in the cluster and installing the binaries on that shared file system (read the next chapter for more details on how to do this). Alternatively, you can just install the binaries on all cluster nodes that need to be able to run them.

---

1. Log in to one of the cluster nodes, either as user root or as user hacluster.

2. Type the crm command and then ra. From there, type list ocf, to display a list of all OCF resource agents. Browse through the list and verify that you see the IPaddr2, Filesystem, and apache resource agents.

3. Still from the crm ra environment, type meta IPaddr2, to show a list of parameters that can be used by the IPaddr resource agents. Listing 6-1 shows what the output of this command may look like. With this procedure, we are going to use the following parameters. Read through the explanation of how to use these resource agents.

- ip: The IP address that is going to be used for the resource you're adding to the cluster.

- cidr_netmask: The cidr netmask that is used in your IP network, that is, 24 and not 255.255.255.0

Listing 6-1. Displaying RA Properties

```
Manages virtual IPv4 addresses (Linux specific version) (ocf:heartbeat:IPaddr2)

This Linux-specific resource manages IP alias IP addresses.
It can add an IP alias, or remove one.
In addition, it can implement Cluster Alias IP functionality
if invoked as a clone resource.

Parameters (* denotes required, [] the default):

ip* (string): IPv4 address
    The IPv4 address to be configured in dotted quad notation, for example
    "192.168.1.1".

nic (string): Network interface
    The base network interface on which the IP address will be brought
    online.

    If left empty, the script will try and determine this from the
    routing table.

    Do NOT specify an alias interface in the form eth0:1 or anything here;
    rather, specify the base interface only.

    Prerequisite:

    There must be at least one static IP address, which is not managed by
    the cluster, assigned to the network interface.

    If you can not assign any static IP address on the interface,
    modify this kernel parameter:
    sysctl -w net.ipv4.conf.all.promote_secondaries=1
    (or per device)
```

4. You now have to find out the attributes for the file system. Still from the `crm ra` environment, type `meta Filesystem` and read the help that is provided. To create a resource for the file system on the shared storage device, you'll have to use the following parameters:

- `device`: This is the name of the block device you want to mount. Make sure to choose a persistent name. A device name such as `/dev/sdb` is dynamically generated and may change. Better use a name that is based on device properties that won't change, such as the names that are created in the `/dev/disk` directory.

- `directory`: This is the directory with which you want to mount the shared storage device. In the case of an Apache web server, it makes sense to use the DocumentRoot stanza from the Apache configuration file as the directory (`/srv/www/htdocs` on SUSE, `/var/www/html` on Red Hat). Note that, normally, it is recommended to use a specific instance and not the system-wide web server.

- `fstype`: This is the file system type that you've formatted the shared storage device with.

As you can see, the parameters that you'll be using to create a file system resource are the same parameters as the ones you'll use when mounting a file system manually.

5. Next, you must find the properties that are going to be assigned to the apache OCF resource. From the `crm resource` prompt, if you use `meta ocf:apache` to display a list of parameters, you'll notice that there are no mandatory parameters for this resource. You'll also notice that many parameters can be managed by the cluster, such as the Apache configuration file. This is useful if you want to take out certain parameters from the regular location and store it on the shared storage device.

Before making your final selection for the Apache resource, you should consider that there are two ways to create that resource. You can use the OCF resource, and you can use the LSB, or service resource. The difference is that the OCF resource manages many Apache properties from the cluster, whereas the LSB, or service resource, is only capable of starting and stopping the resource.

6. Based on the information you've received in the previous three steps, you can now add the resources and their configuration to the cluster. So, enter the command `crm configure edit` and add configuration to the end of the configuration file, as in Listing 6-2.

Listing 6-2. Adding Resources for the Apache Server to the Cluster

```
primitive fs-apache ocf:heartbeat:Filesystem \
        params fstype="xfs" device="/dev/sda1" directory="/srv/www/htdocs" \
        op stop interval="0" timeout="60" \
        op start interval="0" timeout="60" \
        op monitor interval="20" timeout="40" \
        meta target-role="Started"
primitive ip-apache ocf:heartbeat:IPaddr2 \
        params cidr_netmask="24" ip="192.168.122.40" \
        op stop interval="0" timeout="20s" \
        op start interval="0" timeout="20s" \
        op monitor interval="10s" timeout="20s"
primitive service-apache-1 ocf:heartbeat:apache \
        op stop interval="0" timeout="60" \
        op start interval="0" timeout="60" \
        op monitor interval="20" timeout="40"
```

7. After adding the configuration to the cluster, type `crm_mon`, to verify that the resource is properly activated. If you're having problems activating the resources in the cluster, read Chapter 8, for tips about troubleshooting. If all is well, the `crm_mon` output should look like Listing 6-3. Note that this is not the recommended way of setting things up, because there are dependencies between the different primitives. To make sure all comes up in the right order, use grouping, as explained later in this chapter.

Listing 6-3. Verifying Successful Resource Loading

```
============
Last updated: Sat Apr 26 06:32:51 2014
Last change: Sat Apr 26 06:29:53 2014 by hacluster via crmd on node2
Stack: openais
Current DC: node1 - partition with quorum
Version: 1.1.6-b988976485d15cb702c9307df55512d323831a5e
2 Nodes configured, 2 expected votes
4 Resources configured.
============


Online: [ node1 node2 ]

kvm-stonith       (stonith:external/libvirt):    Started node1
ip-apache         (ocf::heartbeat:IPaddr2):      Started node2
fs-apache         (ocf::heartbeat:Filesystem):   Started node1
service-apache-1  (ocf::heartbeat:apache):       Started node2
```

In the sample code from the previous procedure, you can see that a resource definition consists of several lines. The first line defines the name of the resources and the resource agent that has to be used. After that comes a line that defines the parameters of the resource, like the `cidr_netmask` and the `ip` address parameters for the IP address. Following that are three lines that define the operations that this resource should use. These define how the resource should be stopped, started, and monitored.

Note that instead of entering the configuration in the editor interface, the resources could have been entered one by one from the command line. This offers the advantage that tab completion provides for further parameters and help as to what any specific parameter implies. If, however, you want to be able to base the new configuration on existing lines in the configuration, you might be better off using the editor interface, as discussed here, anyway.

Defining Operations

When adding a resource to the cluster, it is important to properly define how the resource should be started, stopped, and monitored. If a resource normally takes time to come up, you need to give it the appropriate time in the cluster as well. This is done by defining a time-out for stopping and starting the resource. The following two lines give a resource 60 seconds to start and 60 seconds to stop:

```
op stop interval="0" timeout="60" \
op start interval="0" timeout="60" \
```

If the resource cannot start within the start time-out interval, the cluster will draw the conclusion that the resource doesn't run on this node and try to start it somewhere else. (This behavior may be modified by adjusting the `start-is-fatal` property. In addition, it will stop the resource first.) If the resource doesn't stop within the time-out of 60 seconds, the cluster will by default force it to a halt via STONITH, with all the associated possible negative consequences. Therefore, it is very important to measure the time it takes to start and stop the resource, by starting it outside of the cluster as a stand-alone application. Next, make sure that your cluster has more than enough time to respect these time-out values!

Another important operation is the monitor operation. This defines how often the cluster should check if the resource is still available. The time-out defines the period of time the cluster should wait before attempting the first monitoring action. The interval defines once every how many seconds (or minutes or hours) the cluster should check whether the resource is still available. If you need your cluster to be responsive, make sure to use low-interval values.

Grouping Resources

If resources should always be together, you have to tell the cluster. If you don't tell the cluster anything, it will load balance the resources. That means that it will evenly distribute the resources among the nodes in the cluster. In the previous procedure, you added resources for an IP address, a file system, and an Apache web service. Now let's have a look at what their current state could look like (see Listing 6-4).

Listing 6-4. Showing Current Resource State

```
Last updated: Tue Feb  4 13:03:02 2014
Last change: Tue Feb  4 13:02:57 2014 by root via cibadmin on node2
Stack: classic openais (with plugin)
Current DC: node1 - partition with quorum
Version: 1.1.9-2db99f1
2 Nodes configured, 2 expected votes
4 Resources configured.


Online: [ node1 node2 ]

stonith-libvirt   (stonith:external/libvirt):    Started node1
ip-apache         (ocf::heartbeat:IPaddr2):      Started node2
fs-apache         (ocf::heartbeat:Filesystem):   Started node1
service-apache-1  (ocf::heartbeat:apache):       Started node1

    Failed actions:

service-apache-1_start_0 (node=node2, call=26, rc=5, status=complete): not i
nstalled
```

As you can see, the IP address is hosted by node1, where the file system and the Apache service are hosted by node2. That means that all connections come in on an IP address that doesn't have an Apache service behind it. So, this configuration isn't going to work, as all resources should be kept together!

There are two solutions that ensure that resources are always together. The easiest and recommended solution is to work with groups. Resources in a group are always kept together on the same node, and they will also be started in the order in which they are listed in the group. In the case of our Apache web service, this is also important, because the IP address and the file system have to be available at the moment the Apache service itself is starting. Creating a group is relatively easy. You just have to add one line into the cluster configuration in which you define the group name and the names of the resources you want to put in the group.

1. Make sure you are logged in as root or user hacluster on one of the cluster nodes.

2. Type crm configure edit and add the following line:

    ```
    group apache-group ip-apache fs-apache service-apache-1
    ```

Alternatively, you can type crm configure group apache-group ip-apache fs-apache service-apache-1 directly from the command line. When typing directly from the command line, you can use tab-completion for the group's members.

3. Close the editor to save and apply the changes and use crm_mon to verify that the resources are now started from a resource group. In the output of crm_mon, you can see the name of the group, as well as the resources that are configured in that group (see Listing 6-5).

Listing 6-5. Monitoring Resources in a Group

```
============
Last updated: Sat Apr 26 06:36:53 2014
Last change: Sat Apr 26 06:35:55 2014 by root via cibadmin on node1
Stack: openais
Current DC: node1 - partition with quorum
Version: 1.1.6-b988976485d15cb702c9307df55512d323831a5e
2 Nodes configured, 2 expected votes
4 Resources configured.
============

Online: [ node1 node2 ]

kvm-stonith      (stonith:external/libvirt):      Started node1
 Resource Group: apache-group
     ip-apache   (ocf::heartbeat:IPaddr2):        Started node2
     fs-apache   (ocf::heartbeat:Filesystem):     Started node2
     service-apache-1   (ocf::heartbeat:apache):  Started node2
```

Working with Constraints

A resource group is a convenient way of keeping resources together. If you have a complex dependency, however, a group is not the best possible way to define that. If the dependencies are becoming more complex, you're better off using constraints. A constraint is a set of rules that defines how resources should be loaded.

Constraint Types

Over time, some less common constraint types have been added, but the most important constraint types are the following:

- *Location*: A location constraint defines on which server a resource should be loaded. You can also use it to define locations where the resource may never be loaded.

- *Colocation*: A colocation constraint is used to define what specific resources should be loaded together or, alternatively, that they should never be loaded together.

- *Order*: An order constraint is used to define a specific order. Order constraints are implicit in resource groups, but using order constraints may be more convenient, as you can define these between different types of resources. You could, for example, define that a resource group can only be loaded after some specific primitive has been loaded first.

Understanding Scores

When working with constraints, you can define priorities. To define priorities, scores are used. On every constraint, you can use a score from -1,000,000 (-INFINITY) up to INFINITY (1,000,000), and you can use every value in between.

To express that you never want a certain action to be performed, you can use a negative score. Any score smaller than 0 will ban the resource from a node.

Let's have a look at a sample cluster to understand this better. In the sample cluster, four nodes are used: node1, node2, node3, and node4. You want a resource group with the name db-group to be loaded by preference on node1 or node2. If it cannot be loaded on either, it should be loaded on node3, but it should never load on node4. To express this in scores, you might assign a score of 100,000 to node1 and node2, a score of 1,000 to node3, and a score of -INFINITY to node4.

You can, of course, create constraints from the crm shell, but as the syntax can be a bit complex, I recommend using the Hawk interface to define them. The following procedure explains how to do this.

1. Log in to the Hawk interface, and from the button bar on the left, click Constraints. This will show the three different constraints that are available.

2. Select Location and click + to add a new constraint. This opens the interface that you can see in Figure 6-1.

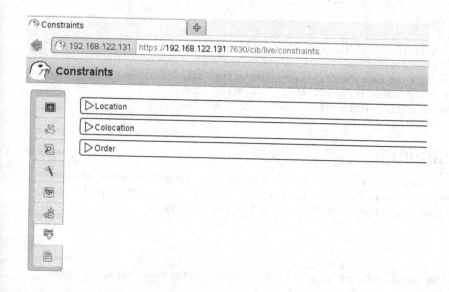

Figure 6-1. *Creating new constraints*

3. Enter a constraints ID, and from the Resource drop-down list, select the `apache-group` you've just created.

4. At this point, you can simply enter a score and the node where you want this resource to be running on, but you can also add a more complex constraint, by selecting the Show Rule Editor box. This opens a new interface that you can see in Figure 6-2. If you want to configure more complex constraints, you need the rule editor. Let's assume we want the apache-group to have a preference for node1 and node2, and, only if it's not possible to run it on these, it should run on node3, and at the same time, it should never run on node4.

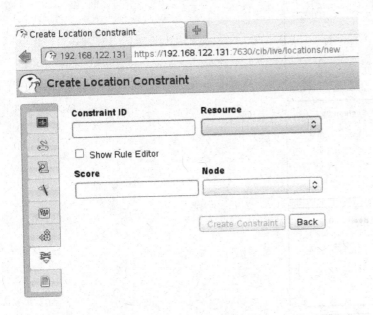

Figure 6-2. *Working with the constraint rule editor*

5. In the rule editor, enter a score of 100000 and then define the expression #uname (which refers to the kernel node name of the node), = node1. If you would like to add another node with the same score, you can specify this node directly under the first expression (see Figure 6-3).

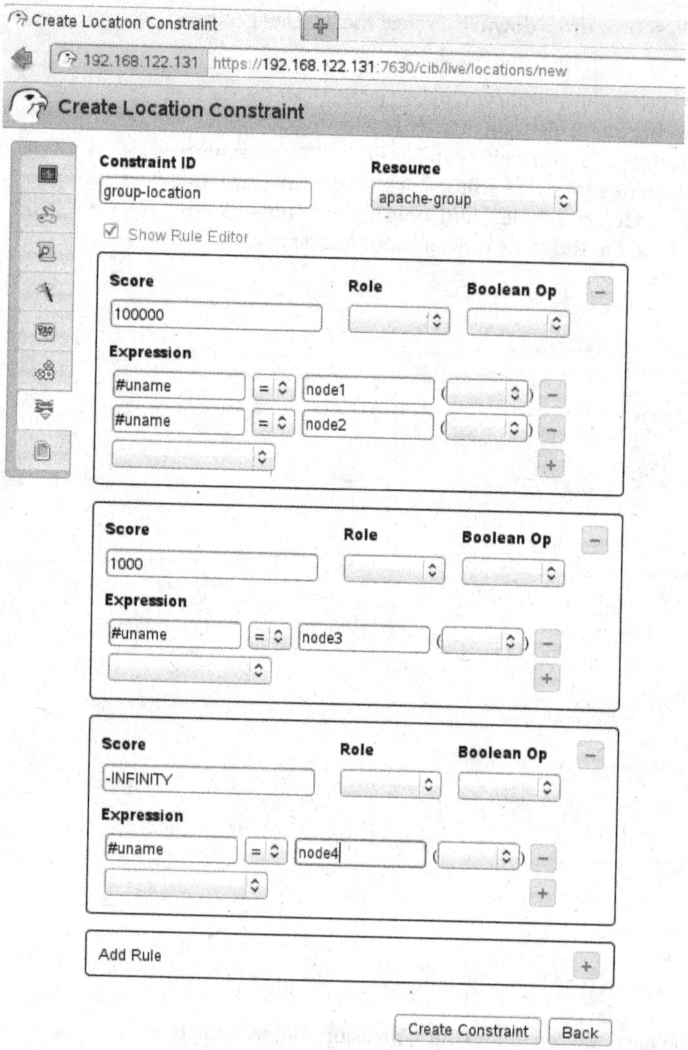

Figure 6-3. *Configuring complex constraints*

6. To add a node with a lower score, click + and enter a score of 1000. Now add the expression for node3. Next, you can add another rule with a score of -INFINITY that relates to node4.

After creating the constraint, it is visible from the `crm configure edit` interface as well, and you can modify it at will from the following interface:

```
location group-location apache-group \
        rule $id="group-location-rule" 100000: #uname eq node1 and #uname eq node2 \
        rule $id="group-location-rule-0" 1000: #uname eq node3 \
        rule $id="group-location-rule-1" -inf: #uname eq node4
```

Note that in the example discussed previously, location constraints are used. In many cases, use of these is not necessary. If the nodes are symmetric, the cluster can find out for itself how to place resources. Alternatively, utilization parameters can be used to make placement decisions. In these, the node as well as the resources can be configured with utilization information.

In more complex setups, users may have to specify ordering and colocation, and possibly resource priorities, to arbitrate capacity shortages or conflicts between anti-colocated resources.

Testing the Configuration

At this point, it's time to subject the configuration to a test. If the node that is currently hosting the Apache group goes down, the other node should automatically take over, and the failing node should be terminated by a STONITH operation.

1. Make sure you can see the console of both nodes and find out where the apache-group is currently running. Log in as root on the other node and start the command crm_mon here.

2. On the node that currently hosts the apache-group, use the command echo c > /proc/sysrq-trigger to crash the node. Watch what is happening in crm_mon. You should see that the resources are migrated over to the other node.

3. At the moment the failing node comes back, you will see it appearing in the cluster, and you'll notice that the resource group automatically fails back to the original node.

Normally, your cluster should work fine at the moment. If it doesn't, read the Chapter 8, in which you will find some important troubleshooting tips.

Understanding Resource Agent Scripts

In this chapter's previous sections, you have learned how to create resources in a cluster. Behind these resources are the resource agents, which are scripts that tell the cluster how to deal with the clustered services. An OCF resource agent is a shell script, enriched with some XML code, and as an administrator, you can create these scripts yourself. In this section, we'll explore the structure of an RA script, to help you in developing your own RAs.

To understand how a resource agent script is made, the Dummy RA provides a good example that is not too long. Use find / -name "Dummy" to find the exact location (/usr/lib/ocf/resource.d/heartbeat/Dummy on SUSE). In Listing 6-6, you can see what its contents looks like (cleaned up a little bit, so as not to make it too long).

Listing 6-6. Sample RA Script

```
node1:/usr/lib/ocf/resource.d/heartbeat # cat Dummy
#!/bin/sh
#
#
#       Dummy OCF RA. Does nothing but wait a few seconds, can be
#       configured to fail occasionally.
#
# Copyright (c) 2004 SUSE LINUX AG, Lars Marowsky-Brée
#                    All Rights Reserved.
#
# This program is free software; you can redistribute it and/or modify
# it under the terms of version 2 of the GNU General Public License as
# published by the Free Software Foundation.
#
....
```

81

```
#######################################################################
# Initialization:

: ${OCF_FUNCTIONS_DIR=${OCF_ROOT}/lib/heartbeat}
. ${OCF_FUNCTIONS_DIR}/ocf-shellfuncs

#######################################################################

meta_data() {
        cat <<END
<?xml version="1.0"?>
<!DOCTYPE resource-agent SYSTEM "ra-api-1.dtd">
<resource-agent name="Dummy" version="0.9">
<version>1.0</version>

<longdesc lang="en">
This is a Dummy Resource Agent. It does absolutely nothing except
keep track of whether its running or not.
Its purpose in life is for testing and to serve as a template for RA writers.

NB: Please pay attention to the timeouts specified in the actions
section below. They should be meaningful for the kind of resource
the agent manages. They should be the minimum advised timeouts,
but they shouldn't/cannot cover _all_ possible resource
instances. So, try to be neither overly generous nor too stingy,
but moderate. The minimum timeouts should never be below 10 seconds.
</longdesc>
<shortdesc lang="en">Example stateless resource agent</shortdesc>

<parameters>
<parameter name="state" unique="1">
<longdesc lang="en">
Location to store the resource state in.
</longdesc>
<shortdesc lang="en">State file</shortdesc>
<content type="string" default="${HA_RSCTMP}/Dummy-${OCF_RESOURCE_INSTANCE}.state" />
</parameter>

<parameter name="fake" unique="0">
<longdesc lang="en">
Fake attribute that can be changed to cause a reload
</longdesc>
<shortdesc lang="en">Fake attribute that can be changed to cause a reload</shortdesc>
<content type="string" default="dummy" />
</parameter>

</parameters>
```

```
<actions>
<action name="start"          timeout="20" />
<action name="stop"           timeout="20" />
<action name="monitor"        timeout="20" interval="10" depth="0" />
<action name="reload"         timeout="20" />
<action name="migrate_to"     timeout="20" />
<action name="migrate_from"   timeout="20" />
<action name="meta-data"      timeout="5" />
<action name="validate-all"   timeout="20" />
</actions>
</resource-agent>
END
}


#####################################################################


dummy_usage() {
        cat <<END
usage: $0 {start|stop|monitor|migrate_to|migrate_from|validate-all|meta-data}

    Expect to have a fully populated OCF RA-compliant environment set.

END
}

dummy_start() {
    dummy_monitor
    if [ $? = $OCF_SUCCESS ]; then
        return $OCF_SUCCESS
    fi
    touch ${OCF_RESKEY_state}
}

dummy_stop() {
    dummy_monitor
    if [ $? = $OCF_SUCCESS ]; then
        rm ${OCF_RESKEY_state}
    fi
    return $OCF_SUCCESS
}

dummy_monitor() {
        # Monitor _MUST!_ differentiate correctly between running
        # (SUCCESS), failed (ERROR) or _cleanly_ stopped (NOT RUNNING).
        # That is THREE states, not just yes/no.

        if [ -f ${OCF_RESKEY_state} ]; then
            return $OCF_SUCCESS
```

```
        fi
        if false ; then
                return $OCF_ERR_GENERIC
        fi
        return $OCF_NOT_RUNNING
}

dummy_validate() {

    # Is the state directory writable?
    state_dir=`dirname "$OCF_RESKEY_state"`
    touch "$state_dir/$$"
    if [ $? != 0 ]; then
        return $OCF_ERR_ARGS
    fi
    rm "$state_dir/$$"

    return $OCF_SUCCESS
}

: ${OCF_RESKEY_state=${HA_RSCTMP}/Dummy-${OCF_RESOURCE_INSTANCE}.state}
: ${OCF_RESKEY_fake="dummy"}

case $__OCF_ACTION in
meta-data)      meta_data
                exit $OCF_SUCCESS
                ;;
start)          dummy_start;;
stop)           dummy_stop;;
monitor)        dummy_monitor;;
migrate_to)     ocf_log info "Migrating ${OCF_RESOURCE_INSTANCE} to ${OCF_RESKEY_CRM_meta_migrate_
target}."
                dummy_stop
                ;;
migrate_from)   ocf_log info "Migrating ${OCF_RESOURCE_INSTANCE} from ${OCF_RESKEY_CRM_meta_migrate_
source}."
                dummy_start
                ;;
reload)         ocf_log info "Reloading ${OCF_RESOURCE_INSTANCE} ..."
                ;;
validate-all)   dummy_validate;;
usage|help)     dummy_usage
                exit $OCF_SUCCESS
                ;;
*)              dummy_usage
                exit $OCF_ERR_UNIMPLEMENTED
                ;;
esac
rc=$?
ocf_log debug "${OCF_RESOURCE_INSTANCE} $__OCF_ACTION : $rc"
exit $rc
```

As you can see, the script consists of several parts. In the first part, an include file with the name `ocf-shellfuncs` is called. This input script file defines several functions that are available in OCF scripts. Make sure it is included if ever you want to write your own RA script.

Second, there is a somewhat longer section containing metadata. This metadata is in XML format, and it is what is displayed when using a command such as `crm ra meta`. It also contains the default values that are used for this resource type, if not defined otherwise.

Next, the valid arguments are defined. As you can see, such common arguments as `start` and `stop` are defined. Also, the cluster-specific variables are defined here. Later on in the script, these arguments are further defined in bash functions, with the task that should be accomplished when one of these actions is called. The last part of the script defines a `case` loop, where all of the arguments can be called from.

As you can see, the way an RA script is structured is not that complicated. Just make sure that it contains the parts that are described previously, and you can clusterize anything you'd like. If you have to create your own RA scripts, it's a good idea to start from the Dummy script as a sample and work that out to provide all the functionality you require. For more information about developing resource agents, I'd recommend you consult "OCF Resource Agent Developer's Guide" by Florian Haas at `www.linux-ha.org/doc/dev-guides/ra-dev-guide.html`.

Summary

In this chapter, you have learned how to work with resources in the cluster. You have learned how to create primitives and how to put several primitives together in a group resource. You've also read about how to use constraints to define complex rules between primitives. In the next chapter, you'll learn how to work with storage in a clustered environment.

CHAPTER 7

███

Clustering Storage

When working with cluster resources for services, these services typically require access to files as well. In a cluster environment, you can work with the filesystem resource to have a file system mount run on the nodes where you need it. There's more to clustered file systems, though. In this chapter, you'll learn how to configure your cluster for shared file systems.

Using a Cluster File System

In some cases, it makes sense to use a cluster-aware file system. The purpose of a cluster-aware file system is to allow multiple nodes to write to the file system simultaneously. The default cluster-aware file system on the SUSE Linux Enterprise Server is OCFS2, and on Red Hat, it is Global File System (GFS) 2. The file system is doing this by synchronizing caches between the nodes that have the filesystem resource running immediately, which means that every node always has the actual state of exactly what is happening on the file system.

To create a cluster-aware file system, you need two supporting services. The first of these is the distributed lock manager, dlm. The second is o2cb, which takes care of the communication of the OCFS2 file system with the cluster. (Note that for starting SLES 12, only the DLM service is required, and the o2cb service is no longer needed.) As with the OCFS2 file system itself, these resources have to be started on all nodes that require access to the file system. Pacemaker provides the clone resource for this purpose. Clone resorts can be applied for any resources that have to be activated on multiple nodes simultaneously.

Although cluster-aware file systems may sound useful, you don't need them in all cases. Typically, you'll need them in active/active scenarios, where multiple instances of the same resource are running on multiple nodes and are all active. You don't have to create a cluster file system, if you only want to run one instance of a resource at the same time.

Apart from the benefits, there are also disadvantages to using cluster file systems. The most important disadvantage is that the cache has to be synchronized between all nodes involved. This makes a cluster file system slower than a stand-alone file system, in many cases, especially those that involve a lot of metadata operations. Because they also provide much stronger coupling between the nodes, it becomes harder for the cluster to prevent faults from spreading.

It is often believed that a cluster file system provides an advantage over failover times, as compared to a local node file system, because it is already mounted. However, this is not true; the file system is still paused until fencing/STONITH and journal recovery for the failed node have completed. This will freeze the clustered file system on *all* nodes. It is actually a set of independent local file systems that provides higher availability! Clustered file systems should be used where they are required, but only after careful planning.

Configuring an OCFS2 File System

Before going into detail, it's good to have a generic overview of the procedure that has to be followed to create an OCFS2 file system. The procedure is roughly as follows:

1. Create a resource group containing the dlm and o2cb resources.

2. Put this group in a clone resource, to ensure that it runs on multiple nodes.

3. Start the resource on all nodes that have to use the cluster file system.

4. Use mkfs.ocfs2 to format the OCFS2 file system.

5. Create a clone resource that also mounts the OCFS2 file system.

Understanding Clone Resources

When working with a clustered file system, the file system must be started on multiple nodes in the cluster. To accomplish this, you need a special resource type: the clone resource type. Working with clones is not so hard. You'll first create primitive resources and, next, configure a clone to run the primitives on multiple nodes simultaneously. While creating the clone, you'll define properties that specify how often the resource should be started.

The OCFS2 file system depends on two generic processes that have to be loaded on each OCFS2 node. The first is the distributed lock manager control daemon. This is the dlm controld process that will be created as a clone resource. This process is used by cLVM2 (see later in this chapter) and OCFS2, and it coordinates locks between cluster nodes.

The second process that OCFS2 depends on is o2cb, the OCFS2 cluster base. This is the software that tells OCFS2 how to find the cluster. In this case, a pacemaker cluster is used, but OCFS2 can be configured with its own cluster stack as well. If this is the case, o2cb tells the OCFS2 file system how to find that cluster.

■ **Note** The default configuration for OCFS2 is to use its own cluster stack. If by accident you format an OCFS2 file system while the o2cb module is not present, you'll receive a cluster communications error. To fix that, you can use the tune2fs.ocfs2 command. If that doesn't work, you will have to format the OCFS2 file system again, while the o2cb module is running.

The detailed procedure for creating an OCFS2 file system resource is described below.

1. Type crm configure edit and add the following primitives:

```
primitive dlm ocf:pacemaker:controld \
        op start interval="0" timeout="90" \
        op stop interval="0" timeout="100" \
        op monitor interval="10" timeout="20" start-delay="0"
primitive o2cb ocf:ocfs2:o2cb \
        op stop interval="0" timeout="100" \
        op start interval="0" timeout="90" \
        op monitor interval="20" timeout="20"
```

2. Create a group that contains the two primitives you've just added, by adding the following line as well:

```
group ocfs2-base-group dlm o2cb
```

3. At this point, you can create a clone that contains the group and ensures that the primitives in the group are started on all nodes. While creating the clone, you can consider adding two parameters. The first is clone-max. This parameter tells the clone how many instances of the primitive(s) in the clone should be started. Using this parameter makes sense if you have more nodes in the cluster than the amount of nodes where you want this resource to be active on. If not set, clone-max defaults to the number of nodes in the cluster. The clone-node-max parameter tells the cluster how many instances of a primitive can run on one node. In most cases, you will probably want to set it to one, but on some occasions, it may make sense to run the primitives more than once. An important parameter to consider is interleave="true". By setting this parameter, you make loading resources that have a dependency to some other resources easier. Imagine an order constraint where clone resource B is started after clone resource A. With the interleave setting to false, clone resource B would only start when all instances of resource A had been started. If you set interleave to true, instances of resource B can start loading before resource A has loaded everywhere. The final configuration for the clone with the OCFS2 supporting modules would look as follows:

```
clone ocfs2-base-clone ocfs2-base-group \
        meta interleave="true"
```

4. Write the changes and close the editor. This activates the cloned group immediately.

5. Type crm_mon to verify that the group has been started. The result should look as follows:

```
Last updated: Tue Feb  4 15:43:15 2014
Last change: Tue Feb  4 15:40:24 2014 by root via cibadmin on node1
Stack: classic openais (with plugin)
Current DC: node2 - partition with quorum
Version: 1.1.9-2db99f1
2 Nodes configured, 2 expected votes
8 Resources configured.

Online: [ node1 node2 ]

stonith-libvirt (stonith:external/libvirt):       Started node1
  Resource Group: apache-group
      ip-apache   (ocf::heartbeat:IPaddr2):        Started node1
      fs-apache   (ocf::heartbeat:Filesystem):     Started node1
      service-apache      (ocf::heartbeat:apache): Started node1
  Clone Set: ocfs2-base-clone [ocfs2-base-group]
      Started: [ node1 node2 ]
```

6. As the components that are required to create an OCFS2 file system are operational, you can now proceed and create the OCFS2 file system. Note that you have two options here. By this procedure, you'll create the OCFS2 file system directly on top of a shared disk device. It might make sense, however, to create an LVM2 sub-layer first. This makes it easier to change the size of the file system or to work with other advanced features that are offered by LVM2.

Identify the shared SAN disk on which you want to create the file system. On this disk, use the `mkfs.ocfs2` command `mkfs.ocfs2 /dev/sdb`. (Note that I'm using `/dev/sdb` here only for the purpose of legibility. Use device names that are based on the naming in `/dev/disk/...` to ensure that devices are named persistently.)

7. Create a mount point for the file systems on all nodes involved: `mkdir /shared`.

8. Mount the file system on both nodes and write a file on both nodes. You'll see that the file immediately becomes visible on the other node as well.

9. Use `crm configure edit` to add a primitive for the OCFS2 file system to the cluster. Note that you'll add the file system by using a `filesystem` resource, as you have done previously when adding an Ext3 file system to the cluster.

```
primitive ocfs-fs ocf:heartbeat:Filesystem \
        params fstype="ocfs2" device="/dev/disk/by-path/ip-192.168.1.125:3260-iscsi-
iqn.2014-01.com.example:kiabi" directory="/shared" \
        op stop interval="0" timeout="60" \
        op start interval="0" timeout="60" \
        op monitor interval="20" timeout="40"
```

10. As this is an OCFS2 file system, you probably want to run it on multiple nodes. To do this, put the primitive you've just created in a clone, by adding the following lines to the configuration also:

```
clone ocfs-fs-clone ocfs-fs \
        meta interleave="true"
```

11. To tell the cluster that the `ocfs2-fs-clone` should only be started once the `ocfs2-base-clone` has successfully been started, you also have to add an order constraint.

```
order ocfs2-fs-after-ocfs-base Mandatory: ocfs2-base-clone ocfs-fs
```

Note that in this case, using constraints is the only option to define the relation between the `ocfs2-base` clone and the `ocfs2` clone. This allows you to define a relationship between two resources that are further configured as independent resources. Note the syntax of the order constraint. After defining that it's an order constraint, a name is specified, followed by the score. Using scores is important in order constraints. I've used the constraint setting of Mandatory to make sure that the cluster can stop cleanly. Next, the resources are specified—in the order that they should be loaded.

12. Save the changes and quit editing mode. The cloned file system has been added to the cluster, and you can now start running `active-active` resources on top of it.

LVM2 in Cluster Environments

The Logical Volume Manager (LVM2) offers some advantages to working with storage. In clustered environments, LVM2 can be used as well, but you'll have to use clustered LVM2 to make sure that the state of volume groups and logical volumes is synchronized properly on the cluster. In this section, you'll learn how to set up cLVM2.

To use cLVM2, you need a few supporting resources. The first of these is `dlm`, which you've also used to configure an OCFS2 file system. Apart from that, you need `cLVM2d`, the cluster volume manager daemon. This daemon is used to synchronize LVM2 metadata in the cluster. These modules must be available on all nodes that are going to provide access LVM2 volumes that are managed by the cluster. As they have to be loaded on multiple nodes simultaneously, you have to configure `clone` resources for them.

Once the supporting modules are available, you can create a clustered LVM2 volume group. Note that it is the volume group and not the LVM2 logical volume that is cloned, and you'll first have to create it on the command line of one of the nodes that has dlm and cLVM2d running. After creating the resource for the volume group, you can create LVM2 logical volumes on any of the nodes in the cluster.

After creating these objects at the LVM2 level, you can create a cluster resource that manages the volume group. You only need this resource for the volume group, as it is the volume group that is responsible for managing cluster access to its logical volumes. When creating the volume group, you can also decide whether or not to configure it for exclusive access. By default, all nodes in the cluster can access the clustered volume group, which makes it easy to set up a shared file system like OCFS2 on top of it. If it is configured for exclusive access, it will be locked for all other nodes when it is in use. The procedure below describes how to create a cLVM2 setup.

1. Type crm configure edit and add the following code to the cluster configuration to add primitives for cLVM2d and dlm. Note that you only need to add the dlm primitive if you haven't done that already in the preceding section.

```
primitive cLVM2-base ocf:LVM22:cLVM2d \
        op start interval="0" timeout="90" \
        op stop interval="0" timeout="100" \
        op monitor interval="20" timeout="20"
primitive dlm ocf:pacemaker:controld \
        op start interval="0" timeout="90" \
        op stop interval="0" timeout="100" \
        op monitor interval="10" timeout="20" start-delay="0"
```

2. As the resources need to be configured as clones, you need to add the clones as well. Note that in the following sample code, the target-role is set to Stopped. This is because the cLVM2-clone can only be started after the dlm-clone. If you don't do anything, the cluster will bring up the resources, and you risk the cLVM2-clone being started before the dlm-clone, in which case it fails. To prevent this, we'll add it to the cluster in Stopped mode first and start the resource manually in the next step, to bring them up in the right order. As a permanent, fix we'll add an order constraint later.

```
clone dlm-clone dlm \
        meta target-role="Stopped" interleave="true"
clone cLVM2-clone cLVM2-base \
        meta target-role="Stopped" interleave="true"
```

3. Write and commit the changes to the cluster.

4. Type crm resource start dlm-clone; crm resource start cLVM2-clone. This should start both clones in the cluster. Don't proceed before you have confirmed that the clones have indeed been started.

```
Last updated: Fri Feb  7 13:47:26 2014
Last change: Fri Feb  7 07:37:53 2014 by hacluster via crmd on node1
Stack: classic openais (with plugin)
Current DC: node2 - partition with quorum
Version: 1.1.9-2db99f1
2 Nodes configured, 2 expected votes
15 Resources configured.
```

```
Online: [ node1 node2 ]

ip-test                (ocf::heartbeat:IPaddr2):      Started node1
ip-test-encore         (ocf::heartbeat:IPaddr2):      Started node2
sbd-stonith            (stonith:external/sbd):        Started node1
 Resource Group: apache-group
     ip-apache         (ocf::heartbeat:IPaddr2):      Started node2
     fs-apache         (ocf::heartbeat:Filesystem):   Started node2
     service-apache    (ocf::heartbeat:apache):       Started node2
 Clone Set: dlm-clone [dlm]
     Started: [ node1 node2 ]
 Clone Set: ocfs2-clone [ocfs2-group]
     Started: [ node1 node2 ]
```

5. Open the file /etc/lvm/lvm.conf. Look for the parameter lock_mode and make sure it has the value 3.

6. At this point, you can create the LVM2 volume group on the command line of one of the nodes, with the cluster property enabled. The only requirement is that shared storage needs to be available. Assuming that the shared disk device is available on both nodes as /dev/sdd, use the following command to create the clustered volume group:

    ```
    vgcreate -c y vgcluster /dev/sdd
    ```

With this command, you create a volume group with the name vgcluster that is based on the /dev/sdd shared disk device.

You should note that in this example, the /dev/sdd device name is used. In this case, that is no problem. The vgcreate command writes metadata to the device, and this metadata will be scanned when the reboot comes up. Even if the device name changes, for instance, from /dev/sdd to /dev/sde, the metadata will be found anyway, and the vg name that is in the metadata won't change.

7. Now you can create the LVM2 logical volume. To create an LVM2 volume that consumes all disk space that is available in the volume group, use the following command:

    ```
    lvcreate -n lvcluster -l 100%FREE vgcluster
    ```

8. Type lvs to verify that the volume group and the LVM2 logical volume have been created.

    ```
    node2:~ # lvs
      LV        VG        Attr       LSize   Pool Origin Data% Move Log Copy% Convert
      lvcluster vgcluster -wi-a---- 508.00m
    ```

9. You now have to define a cluster resource that is going to manage access to the volume group. Use crm configure edit vgcluster and enter the following lines:

    ```
    primitive vgcluster ocf:heartbeat:LVM2 \
            params volgrpname="vgcluster" \
            op start interval="0" timeout="30" \
            op stop interval="0" timeout="30" \
            op monitor interval="10" timeout="30"
    ```

10. As the primitive that manages access to the clustered volume group needs to be available on all nodes where the logical volumes can be accessed, you have to put it in a clone before starting it. To do this, type `crm configure edit vgcluster-clone` and add the following lines:

```
clone vgcluster-clone vgcluster \
        meta target-role="Started" interleave="true"
```

11. Write and quit the cluster editor, which automatically commits the new volume group resource to the cluster. Type `crm resource status vgcluster-clone` to verify the current status of the newly created resource. If all went well, you'll see that it has been started on both nodes.

```
node1:~ # crm resource status vgcluster-clone
resource vgcluster-clone is running on: node1
resource vgcluster-clone is running on: node2
```

12. Type lvs on both nodes to verify the availability of the logical volumes. You should see them listed on both nodes.

In many cases, the procedure described previously will work fine. Sometimes it won't (see the following code listing).

```
Clone Set: vgcluster-clone [vgcluster]
     Started: [ node2 ]
     Stopped: [ vgcluster:1 ]
```

Failed actions:

```
vgcluster_start_0 (node=node1, call=68, rc=1, status=complete): unknown error
```

If a failure has occurred, you should analyze log files and find out why it occurred and fix it. After analyzing the error and fixing the possible cause, you can stop the clone, clean up its status, and start it again. The following procedure describes how you can do that:

1. Type `crm resource stop vgcluster-clone` and wait for this to complete. Consider adding the option `-w` to the `crm` command, which has the `crm` wait for every preceding step to complete before going on to the next step.

2. Type `crm resource cleanup vgcluster-clone` to remove the current status attributes. This will remove the memory of the resource, which allows it to try to start on all nodes again, without having the memory that it was unsuccessful to start on some of them.

3. Use `crm start vgcluster-clone` to start the resource again.

4. Type `crm resource status vgcluster-clone` to verify the status of the resource. You should see it running without any errors on all of its nodes now.

```
node2:~ # crm resource status vgcluster-clone
resource vgcluster-clone is running on: node2
resource vgcluster-clone is running on: node1
```

At this point, you will have working resources. You can start creating file systems on the LVM2 volumes in the clustered volume group. However, when you reboot a node, starting these resources may fail. This is because nothing has been defined about the startup order between the `cLVM2-clone`, the `dlm-clone`, and the `vgcluster-clone`.

In the previous section, you have learned that you can create a group to keep resources together and have them started in the right order. In some cases, you cannot put resources in a group, and constraints are needed to define how resources should be started.

Imagine that you have an OCFS2 file system that is configured directly on top of shared storage, as discussed in the previous section. Imagine that apart from the OCFS2 file system, in the same cluster, you need access to clustered logical volumes as well. Both OCFS2 as well as cLVM2 require controld to be running on the nodes. Unfortunately, you cannot put the same primitive in multiple groups. In addition, you cannot create multiple primitives and run them multiple times on the same node. You have to create a clone that starts controld and two groups: one for the cLVM2 resources and one for the OCFS2 resources. (See Figure 7-1.) Next, you need a rule that defines that controld has to be started first and the groups can be started next.

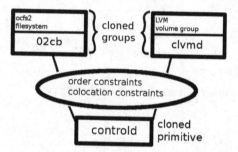

Figure 7-1. *Independent stacks configuration overview*

OCFS2 on Top of cLVM2

As discussed previously, there are different ways in which OCFS2 file systems can be created. Putting OCFS2 on top of cLVM2 volumes offers more options for managing storage, but it also makes managing the cluster stack more complicated. For your convenience, Figure 7-2 gives an overview of the stack that is necessary to run such a configuration.

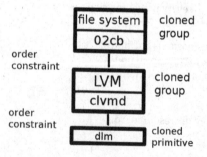

Figure 7-2. *OCFS2 on top of cLVM2 stack overview*

Using GFS2 with Pacemaker

If you're working on a Red Hat cluster, GFS2 is the default cluster file system. The procedure for using GFS2 in a Red Hat cluster is a bit different. The first thing to be aware of is that GFS2 needs to run on top of cLVM2, and in Red Hat Enterprise Linux 6, that only works on top of the cman cluster manager. In Chapter 5, you read how to set up this cluster manager. Once the clustered LVM2 volumes are available on the cluster nodes, you can make the GFS2 file system on top of it. The default Red Hat procedure to do this goes beyond the cluster. That means that you can run mkfs.gfs2 on one of the cluster nodes and take care of the mounts locally: just put a mount line in /etc/fstab to ensure the proper mounting of the GFS2 volume.

Summary

In this chapter, you have read how to configure the cluster with clustered file systems that allow for active/active access to the same files from multiple nodes simultaneously. You have also read how to use cLVM2, which may be useful for stand-alone file systems also. In the next chapter, you'll read about some common cluster management tasks.

■ ■ ■

## CHAPTER 8

Performing Daily Cluster Management Tasks

At this point, your cluster should be operational. That means that your work as a cluster administrator can begin, and you can start managing the cluster resources. All topics in the chapters up to now were mostly about designing the cluster. This chapter is about managing the cluster, and it discusses typical tasks that a cluster administrator might have to perform. The following tasks are discussed:

- Starting and stopping resources
- Monitoring resource state
- Resource migration
- Using resource cleanup
- Managing nodes
- Using unmanaged mode and maintenance mode for maintenance
- Understanding log files
- Backup and restore of the cluster configuration
- Wipe everything and start all over

Starting and Stopping Resources

The most important daily cluster management task is the starting and stopping of resources. Many administrators do not really understand that resources in a cluster are used in a way that is different from resources that run on a local instance of an operating system. Too often, I have seen people trying to temporarily stop a resource using service stop resource or systemctl stop resource. That is so wrong! As the resource is managed by the cluster, the cluster will see that the resource is stopped, and it will immediately start it again, as that is what the cluster was created for! To manage the current state of resources, cluster commands should be used, not local commands.

Starting and stopping resources is easy, from the crm resource interface, just use start resourcename or stop resourcename to start or stop a resource. When using these commands, the meta target-role property is set in the cluster. This property makes sure that the current state of the resource is stored in the cluster, which guarantees that it comes back in the exact same state, if the state of the cluster suddenly changes. That can also lead to some confusion.

Imagine a situation in which a cluster administrator is troubleshooting the current state of a specific resource. Out of despair, he chooses to set the current state of the resource to stopped, using crm resource stop resourcename. Later, he finds out that nothing really helps, and he restarts the entire cluster stack, just to find out that that also didn't help, and the resource is still in a stopped state! So, do always remember that using crm resource start and crm resource stop doesn't just start or stop the resource, it also changes the current state of the resource. So, you might have to undo it on some occasions!

Monitoring Resource State

It may seem obvious, but monitoring the state of resources in the cluster also is an important task. Until now, you have used crm_mon to monitor the current state of the cluster. crm_mon is a useful command, as it refreshes itself automatically, which makes it excellent for monitoring purposes. But it's not ideal in all cases. To understand why, let's have a look at Listing 8-1 and Listing 8-2, which both show the current state of the same cluster.

Listing 8-1. Using crm_mon to Monitor Cluster State

```
Last updated: Sat Apr 26 11:35:47 2014
Last change: Sat Apr 26 11:32:22 2014 by root via cibadmin on node1
Stack: openais
Current DC: node1 - partition with quorum
Version: 1.1.6-b988976485d15cb702c9307df55512d323831a5e
2 Nodes configured, 2 expected votes
10 Resources configured.
============

Online: [ node1 node2 ]

kvm-stonith      (stonith:external/libvirt):      Started node1
 Resource Group: apache-group
     ip-apache   (ocf::heartbeat:IPaddr2):       Started node2
     fs-apache   (ocf::heartbeat:Filesystem):    Started node2
     service-apache-1   (ocf::heartbeat:apache): Started node2
 Clone Set: clvm-clone [clvm-base]
     Started: [ node1 node2 ]
 Clone Set: dlm-clone [dlm]
     Started: [ node1 node2 ]

Failed actions:
    drac-node1_monitor_3600000 (node=node1, call=17045, rc=1, status=complete):
unknown error
    kvm-stonith_monitor_3600000 (node=node1, call=21424, rc=1, status=complete):
unknown error
    drac-node1_monitor_3600000 (node=node2, call=16, rc=-2, status=Timed Out): unknown exec error
```

As you can see, crm_mon gives much detail, including the current state of the cluster, as well as the last errors that have occurred in the cluster (which may be confusing, because even if the error has occurred a long time ago, it still is shown).

crm status also gives useful information. It shows on which node(s) the resources are started, for example:

Listing 8-2. Using crm status to Monitor Cluster Resource State

```
[root@node1 ~]# crm status
Last updated: Mon Jun  9 14:15:12 2014
Last change: Wed May 28 11:54:21 2014 via crm_attribute on node1
Stack: classic openais (with plugin)
Current DC: node2 - partition with quorum
Version: 1.1.10-14.el6_5.2-368c726
2 Nodes configured, 2 expected votes
6 Resources configured


Online: [ node1 node2 ]

 FenceSQ1 (stonith:fence_ipmilan): Started node2
 Resource Group: mysql-group
     mysql-ip  (ocf::heartbeat:IPaddr2): Started node2
     mysql-fs  (ocf::heartbeat:Filesystem): Started node2
     mysql-db  (ocf::heartbeat:mysql): Started node2
     mysql-web (ocf::heartbeat:apache): Started node2
```

The crm resource status (see Listing 8-3) command doesn't show as much information. Many people think that because crm_mon gives so much information, it shows everything you'd ever want to know about the current cluster status. One important piece of information is missing, however. With crm_mon, you cannot see the resources that actually are stopped, whereas crm resource status shows the state of all resources, including the resources that are stopped. Note that the information that is shown with crm [resource] status can also be shown using the appropriate options with crm_mon.

Listing 8-3. Using crm resource status to Monitor Cluster Resource State

```
node1:~ # crm resource status
 kvm-stonith            (stonith:external/libvirt) Started
 Resource Group: apache-group
     ip-apache          (ocf::heartbeat:IPaddr2) Started
     fs-apache          (ocf::heartbeat:Filesystem) Started
     service-apache-1 (ocf::heartbeat:apache) Started
 Clone Set: clvm-clone [clvm-base]
     Started: [ node1 node2 ]
 Clone Set: dlm-clone [dlm]
     Started: [ node1 node2 ]
 Clone Set: vgcluster-clone [vgcluster]
     Stopped: [ vgcluster:0 vgcluster:1 ]
```

If you like graphical interfaces, you can also monitor the current cluster state from Hawk. From Hawk, click the Cluster Monitor icon, to monitor the current state of the cluster. The default view gives a summary of generic properties, the amount of resources that is configured, and the amount of errors that has occurred (see Figure 8-1). From this interface, you can click the links, to get more details. You can also see the last three errors that have occurred in the cluster. Note that this is a historical overview; you can see past error messages that have been fixed a long time ago.

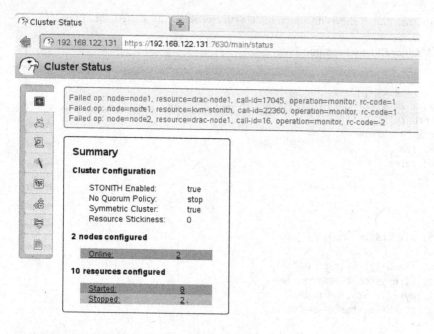

Figure 8-1. *Monitoring cluster state from Hawk*

From Hawk, three different views are offered. If you want to see relations between resources in the cluster, you can activate the tree view from the button in the upper-right part of the screen. This view does give an overview of hierarchical relations of primitives that are configured in groups or clones, but it doesn't show relations that have been defined by use of constraints (see Figure 8-2).

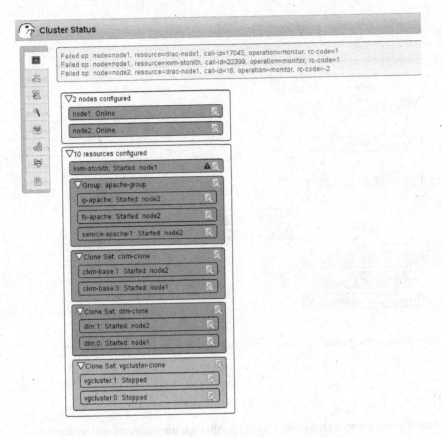

Figure 8-2. *The Hawk tree view shows relations between resources*

If you have to see which resource is running on which node, you can select the Hawk table view, as shown in Figure 8-3. It takes the nodes in your cluster as the starting point and shows all resources running on those nodes.

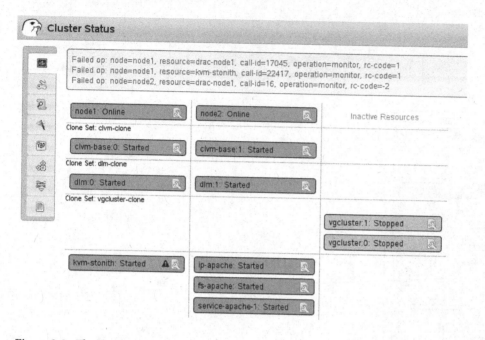

Figure 8-3. *The Hawk table view helps in analyzing which resource is running on which node*

Resource Migration

High availability clusters will take action when a node in the cluster is failing. After failure, resources will be started somewhere else. The cluster can also automatically migrate resources to load balance services across different servers. By default, the cluster tries to evenly balance resources over the nodes in the cluster. This is default behavior, which can be changed by giving the resource stickiness parameter a high positive score.

If you want to prepare for maintenance, you can also perform manual migration actions. By migrating a resource or resource group, you will actually put a location constraint on the resource, preventing the resource from automatically moving back to its original location. Because of this constraint, you should also always un-migrate the resource, or remove the location constraint manually, or specify a "lifetime" for the constraint. This specifies how long the constraint is supposed to stay, after which it would be automatically removed. The next procedure shows how to migrate the apache-group resource toward node1.

1. Type `crm resource status` to show a list of resources and their current status. Note that this doesn't show you the actual node a resource is running on. The `crm_mon` command will do that, if you have to know.

2. Type `crm resource migrate apache-group node1` to migrate the apache-group to node1. Alternatively, the command could be used without mentioning a target node, which follows the current constraint settings to determine where the resource should be migrated to.

3. Now type `crm_mon`, to verify that the migration was successful.

4. Type crm configure show, to display the contents of the current cluster configuration. Note that a location constraint was added to the cluster.

```
location cli-prefer-apache-group apache-group \
        rule $id="cli-prefer-rule-apache-group" inf: #uname eq node1
```

5. Close the editor interface and type crm resource unmigrate apache-group. This removes the location constraint and, depending on the current resource stickiness configuration, might move the resource back to its original location.

In the preceding example, you have seen that manual migration actions place location constraints on resources. These constraints will stick on the resources until you use the crm resource unmigrate command to move the resource back to its original location. Never forget this behavior, as it may cause serious trouble. As you can see in the code snippet, the constraint that has been placed has a score of inf:, which is infinity. That means that the resource will never move back, if the target is still up.

Using Resource Cleanup

If the cluster tries to start a resource on a node, it may encounter problems that make it impossible to start the resource on that node. If that happens, the cluster tries and tries and tries, until the maximum amount of failures has been reached (which normally happens pretty fast). After reaching the maximum amount of failures, the cluster stops trying.

From that moment on, the cluster remembers where it wasn't able to start the resource, which prevents it from trying it again a few moments later. This, however, can lead to a situation in which a resource still thinks it cannot be started somewhere else, whereas the problem may very well have been fixed. If that occurs, you have to clean up the resources (or wait until the failure attributes clean themselves). By applying a cleanup action on a node, resource, or resource group, it will clear its memory of failures and try to do what the cluster wants it to do once more. Using resource cleanup is a very common and important action after fixing problems in the cluster. So, in short, the steps to be taken are as follows:

1. After noticing the failure of a resource to start, fix the problem.

2. Perform a cleanup action.

3. Monitor to see if the cluster is capable of recovering automatically.

The following procedure shows how to perform a cleanup action:

1. Open a crm shell.

2. Type resource to access the resource management interface.

3. Type list to show a list of the resources that are currently active.

4. Type cleanup resourcename to clean up the resource failure properties.

5. Wait a few seconds. The resource should automatically switch back to the state it should be in.

Managing Nodes

When performing maintenance in the cluster, it can be necessary to manage the node status (see Listing 8-4). This should always start with the crm node status command, which shows the status of all nodes in the cluster.

Listing 8-4. Monitoring Node Status

```
crm(live)node# status
<nodes>
  <node id="node1" type="normal" uname="node1">
    <instance_attributes id="nodes-node1">
      <nvpair id="nodes-node1-standby" name="standby" value="off"/>
    </instance_attributes>
  </node>
  <node id="node2" type="normal" uname="node2">
    <instance_attributes id="nodes-node2">
      <nvpair id="nodes-node2-standby" name="standby" value="off"/>
    </instance_attributes>
  </node>
</nodes>
```

If you have to perform maintenance on a node but don't want to bring it down, it's useful to put the node in standby mode. In this mode, the node still counts for quorum, but it won't be a candidate for resources to migrate to. To put a node in standby mode, use the crm node standby nodename command. This adds the standby attribute to the node. To bring a node back to normal operational mode, you can use crm node online nodename. This doesn't remove the standby attribute from the CIB, but it will give the attribute the value off, as you can see in the preceding Listing 8-4.

From the node menu, some other operations are available as well. The most interesting of these is the fence operation. This can be useful for testing your STONITH agent, as this operation will immediately try to fence the node in question. Be careful using this option, because the selected node will be fenced without further notice!

Using Unmanaged Mode and Maintenance Mode for Maintenance

On some occasions, you will have to upgrade the cluster software. If an upgrade requires a restart of the cluster software, you will temporarily loose the resources that are managed by the cluster. Before restarting vital cluster components, resources are moved to another node in the cluster. To avoid that, you can temporarily unmanage a resource. By doing this, you'll temporarily run the resource outside of the cluster, as if it had been started locally. This means that the cluster temporarily doesn't care about the resource status. This allows you to shut down the cluster stack without stopping all resources on it, which is beneficial if you have to perform upgrades on the cluster software.

Once the cluster software is available again, you can manage the resource so that the cluster can take control again. The following procedure shows how to do this:

1. Type crm to open the crm shell.

2. Type resource, followed by status, to see the current state of your resources.

3. Type unmanage apache-group to put the resources in the apache-group in a temporary unmanaged state.

4.   Type status again. You'll see the resources being marked as unmanaged.

5.   Enter the command service openais stop. You'll notice that the node is not
     STONITHed.

6.   Type ps aux | grep http. You will see that the Apache processes are still running.

7.   Put the cluster resource back in a managed state by using the commands service
     openais start, followed by crm resource manage apache-group.

You can set unmanaged as a generic cluster property as well. This temporarily disconnects all resources from the cluster, until you remove the unmanaged attribute. The easiest way to put your entire cluster in unmanaged mode is by adding the is-managed-default=false property to the end of the cluster configuration, using crm configure edit. To verify that the setting has been applied correctly, type crm resource status.

```
crm(live)# resource status
kvm-stonith             (stonith:external/libvirt) Started  (unmanaged) FAILED
Resource Group: apache-group
    ip-apache           (ocf::heartbeat:IPaddr2) Started  (unmanaged)
    fs-apache           (ocf::heartbeat:Filesystem) Started  (unmanaged)
    service-apache-1  (ocf::heartbeat:apache) Started  (unmanaged)
Clone Set: clvm-clone [clvm-base] (unmanaged)
    clvm-base:0         (ocf::lvm2:clvmd) Started  (unmanaged)
    Stopped: [ clvm-base:1 ]
Clone Set: dlm-clone [dlm] (unmanaged)
    dlm:0               (ocf::pacemaker:controld) Started  (unmanaged)
    Stopped: [ dlm:1 ]
Clone Set: vgcluster-clone [vgcluster] (unmanaged)
    Stopped: [ vgcluster:0 vgcluster:1 ]
```

To put the cluster back in managed mode, just remove this line from the cluster configuration. You'll notice that the unmanaged property is removed automatically from all resources in the cluster.

As an alternative to unmanaged mode, you can consider using maintenance mode. When the cluster is in maintenance mode, no operations whatsoever on resources will be attempted by the cluster. To put a cluster in maintenance mode, use crm configure property maintenance-mode=true. You can now start and stop resources and do anything you'd like to do, without having the cluster interfering. There's just one thing to make sure of: you must always enter maintenance mode before starting maintenance tasks on your cluster! Once you're done, you can disable maintenance mode, using crm configure property maintenance-mode=false.

Understanding Log Files

By default, the cluster components send all their log events to syslog. This is directed from the /etc/corosync/corosync.conf file, which contains a logging section stating that log messages are to be sent to the syslog_facility daemon. The results can be overwhelming: even under normal operation, the cluster is rather verbose, which gives great opportunities to analyze if something goes wrong, provided you know what you need to be looking for. In Listing 8-5, you can see a part of the contents of a /var/log/messages file that has been filled by the different parts of the cluster. (Notice that it spans only two seconds of the lifetime of the cluster!)

Listing 8-5. Analyzing Cluster Log Files

```
Apr 26 13:35:08 node1 lrmd: [2746]: info: rsc:kvm-stonith monitor[22618] (pid 32083)
Apr 26 13:35:08 node1 stonith-ng: [2744]: info: stonith_command: Processed st_execute from lrmd:
rc=-1
Apr 26 13:35:08 node1 external/libvirt[32090]: [32101]: ERROR: virsh not installed
Apr 26 13:35:09 node1 stonith: external_status: 'libvirt status' failed with rc 1
Apr 26 13:35:09 node1 stonith: external/libvirt device not accessible.
Apr 26 13:35:09 node1 stonith-ng: [2744]: notice: log_operation: Operation 'monitor' [32084] for
device 'kvm-stonith' returned: -2
Apr 26 13:35:09 node1 stonith-ng: [2744]: ERROR: log_operation: kvm-stonith: Performing: stonith -t
external/libvirt -S
Apr 26 13:35:09 node1 stonith-ng: [2744]: ERROR: log_operation: kvm-stonith: failed:  1
Apr 26 13:35:09 node1 stonith-ng: [2744]: info: stonith_device_execute: Nothing to do for
kvm-stonith
Apr 26 13:35:09 node1 lrm-stonith: [32083]: WARN: map_ra_retvalue: Mapped the invalid return code -2.
Apr 26 13:35:09 node1 lrmd: [2746]: info: operation monitor[22618] on kvm-stonith for client 2750:
pid 32083 exited with return code 1
Apr 26 13:35:09 node1 crmd: [2750]: info: process_lrm_event: LRM operation kvm-stonith_
monitor_3600000 (call=22618, rc=1, cib-update=37034, confirmed=false) unknown error
Apr 26 13:35:09 node1 attrd: [2747]: notice: attrd_trigger_update: Sending flush op to all hosts
for: fail-count-kvm-stonith (4694)
Apr 26 13:35:09 node1 crmd: [2750]: WARN: status_from_rc: Action 3 (kvm-stonith_monitor_3600000) on
node1 failed (target: 0 vs. rc: 1): Error
Apr 26 13:35:09 node1 attrd: [2747]: notice: attrd_perform_update: Sent update 30951: fail-count-
kvm-stonith=4694
Apr 26 13:35:09 node1 crmd: [2750]: WARN: update_failcount: Updating failcount for kvm-stonith on
node1 after failed monitor: rc=1 (update=value++, time=1398533709)
Apr 26 13:35:09 node1 attrd: [2747]: notice: attrd_trigger_update: Sending flush op to all hosts
for: last-failure-kvm-stonith (1398533709)
Apr 26 13:35:09 node1 crmd: [2750]: info: abort_transition_graph: match_graph_event:277
- Triggered transition abort (complete=0, tag=lrm_rsc_op, id=kvm-stonith_monitor_3600000,
magic=0:1;3:13955:0:71bfdf97-aad9-4e7d-924c-9de2dcc30927, cib=0.45.74) : Event failed
Apr 26 13:35:09 node1 attrd: [2747]: notice: attrd_perform_update: Sent update 30953: last-failure-
kvm-stonith=1398533709
Apr 26 13:35:09 node1 crmd: [2750]: info: update_abort_priority: Abort priority upgraded from 0 to 1
Apr 26 13:35:09 node1 crmd: [2750]: info: update_abort_priority: Abort action done superceeded by
restart
Apr 26 13:35:09 node1 crmd: [2750]: info: match_graph_event: Action kvm-stonith_monitor_3600000 (3)
confirmed on node1 (rc=4)
Apr 26 13:35:09 node1 crmd: [2750]: info: abort_transition_graph: te_update_diff:176 - Triggered
transition abort (complete=0, tag=nvpair, id=status-node1-fail-count-kvm-stonith, name=fail-count-
kvm-stonith, value=4694, magic=NA, cib=0.45.75) : Transient attribute: update
Apr 26 13:35:09 node1 crmd: [2750]: info: update_abort_priority: Abort priority upgraded from 1 to
1000000
Apr 26 13:35:09 node1 crmd: [2750]: info: update_abort_priority: 'Event failed' abort superceeded
Apr 26 13:35:09 node1 crmd: [2750]: info: abort_transition_graph: te_update_diff:176 - Triggered
transition abort (complete=0, tag=nvpair, id=status-node1-last-failure-kvm-stonith, name=last-
failure-kvm-stonith, value=1398533709, magic=NA, cib=0.45.76) : Transient attribute: update
```

The benefit of this verbose logging is that everything is in the logs. You'll always be able to find the information you need. The disadvantage is that you may have a hard time finding it, because there's so much information!

Because logging can go really fast, using `tail -f /var/log/messages` is probably not going to help. Messages pass by so quickly, which makes them unreadable. If, however, you apply a filter to your tail, they become a lot more readable. In general, there are two types of information that you might want to grep for: the name of the part of the cluster that generated the log or the name of the service that is unwilling to work correctly in the cluster.

In Listing 8-5, you can easily recognize the different daemons that play a role in the cluster.

- `stonith` and `stonith-ng`: All that is related to fencing

- `lrmd`: The local resource manager daemon, which is responsible for managing resources after receiving the instruction to do so from the `crmd`

- `crmd`: The cluster resource manager daemon, which is responsible for managing all transitions in the cluster

- `attrd`: The attribute daemon, which is responsible for changing status attributes in the cluster

- `pengine`: Responsible for initiating state changes in the cluster

- `cib`: Relates to the Cluster Information Base (CIB), which is the heart of the cluster

- `external`: Relates to external STONITH modules

Understanding what these modules are all about can really help you in troubleshooting. Imagine, for example, that you're having a problem with the apache-group resource. It makes a difference whether you find the problem related to the `crmd`, the `lrmd`, or the `attrd`. If the `crmd` is logging about a problem with your resource, you are probably trying to do something that the cluster doesn't understand. If the `lrmd` is complaining about the resource, then the `crmd` has already agreed to perform the operation, but it cannot be executed by a local machine. If it's the `attrd`, there is a problem changing a status attribute of your resource.

So, if something really doesn't work, use grep on the `/var/log/messages` files, to find information about the resource that isn't doing what it has to, and check which component of the cluster is having problems with it. Once you've isolated the problem in this way, you're probably on the right track to fixing the problem!

Backup and Restore of the Cluster Configuration

Everything that is precious requires a backup. From the `crm` shell, it is relatively easy to create a backup. Use `crm configure save ~/mycluster-$(date +%d-%m-%y).conf` to write a file `mycluster.conf` that has the current date in it. This saves to a file everything you see when using `crm configure edit`. It might be a good idea to perform this command every single day, so that if ever things go wrong, recovery will be easy.

To import configuration from a file, you can use `crm configure load ~/mycluster-somedate.conf` (or whatever the file you want to import is named). This will import all settings in the file you're referring to. You should be aware that it imports all settings, and because it does, it makes sense to do some housekeeping before you start. You have to make sure that you don't try to import resources and other configurations that already exist in the cluster.

In general, there are two methods for using `crm configure load`. You can work with small input files that contain specific resources only—to import only those resources—after making sure that they don't exist any longer in the CIB itself. Or you can choose to wipe the entire cluster configuration first, which allows you to import a previous state of the cluster in an easy way.

Wipe Everything and Start All Over

If you have a good backup (as discussed in the previous section), on some occasions it makes sense to just throw all current configuration away and import a previous configuration that you've already verified. It speaks for itself that you should never, ever do this before making sure that you really have a good backup. If you do, type `cibadmin -E --force`, to wipe everything you've got in the cluster. Next, use `crm configure load ~/mycluster-some-old-and-working-config.conf` to load the old configuration into your Cluster Information Base. This, of course, is only a measure of last resort, if truly nothing else has helped you so far!

Summary

In this chapter, you've read about common cluster management tasks. You've read how to manage the state of individual resources, as well as the state of the entire cluster, to perform day-to-day and not-so-common management tasks. In the next chapter, you'll learn how to create an open source storage area network, using Pacemaker clustering software.

CHAPTER 9

■ ■ ■

Creating an Open Source SAN

Now that you know all about the basic cluster configurations, it's time to have a look at some practical use cases. In this chapter, you'll discover how to create an open source storage area network (SAN) using Pacemaker and related open source software. You'll learn how to configure the following:

- A mirrored network block device with a distributed replicated block device (DRBD)
- An iSCSI target to provide access to the DRBD
- A cluster configuration that manages the location of the active DRBD

Creating an Open Source SAN with Pacemaker

Storage area network (SAN) appliances are for sale for large amounts of money. In some cases, it just doesn't make sense to spent lots of money on a proprietary SAN appliance when you can create an open source SAN solution. Even from a performance perspective, an open source software-based SAN solution doesn't necessarily offer inferior performance. The advantage of working with this type of solution is that many performance-optimization options are available, and you are in no way restricted by the optimizations that can be applied.

The creation of an open source SAN involves roughly two steps: first, you have to configure a distributed replicated block device (DRBD) and have it managed by the cluster. Next, you must configure an iSCSI target and have it follow the master DRBD. This chapter explains in detail how you can do that.

Configuring RAID 1 over the Network with DRBD

If you want to create an environment where multiple nodes can access your data simultaneously, the distributed replicated block device (DRBD) is an excellent choice. This is particularly true if you want to set up a two-node cluster, in which one node must be able to take over the exact state of the other node as fast as possible. The DRBD performs a delta-sync of blocks over the network, which ensures that you'll have the exact same state on different machines in a matter of seconds.

Basically, DRBD is RAID 1 over the network. In the setup that is presented in this chapter, one node behaves as the active node. The other node is standby, but fully synchronized at all times. That means that in case the active node goes down, the standby node can take over immediately. It is possible to set up DRBD without a Pacemaker cluster, but in that case, you would have to switch over active nodes manually if something happened to the node that is currently active. In the setup presented in this chapter, you'll learn how to make switches occur automatically, by integrating the DRBD in a Pacemaker cluster.

One of the good parts of DRBD is that when using it, you don't need an expensive SAN solution. That is because basically, DRBD is your SAN. The basic function of an SAN is to provide a shared device in which access is provided at block level, and that is exactly what DRBD is doing for you. You can even build an additional solution on top of DRBD, in which an iSCSI target is installed on top of DRBD, to implement a mirrored SAN solution. This is not very hard to do, just add an iSCSI target resource in your Pacemaker cluster that follows the DRBD master, as described in this chapter.

Precautionary Measures

The purpose of setting up a DRBD is to create a device that is synchronized over the network. To accomplish this goal, you need two servers, and on both servers, you need a storage device such as a local hard disk—if possible, of the same size on both nodes. It doesn't really matter what you want to use for the shared storage device, many solutions will work. If you can't dedicate a complete disk, you can also use a partition or an LVM logical volume. It doesn't really matter what you're using, as long as it can be addressed as a block device.

In this chapter, I'll work on a dedicated device with the name /dev/vdb that is available on both nodes. After making this device available, you'll have to make sure that the DRBD software is installed as well.

■ **Important!**   The DRBD is likely to synchronize large amounts of data. If this synchronization happens over the same network interface that is used for the cluster traffic, you may hit totem time-outs, with the result that the cluster starts thinking that other nodes are not available. To prevent this from happening, it is very important to separate DRBD synchronization traffic from totem traffic. The best approach is to use a dedicated network for DRBD. If that is not feasible, at least you have to make sure that the totem traffic is using another network interface. Especially in test environments where all is happening on one network interface, it happens too often that cluster time-outs are no longer respected, and nodes are receiving a STONITH because of that!

Creating the Configuration

After installing the software, you can create the DRBD configuration.

To start, we'll assume that you're using two different servers that have the names node1 and node2 and that on those servers, a dedicated hard disk, /dev/vdb, is available as the DRBD. Also, you'll have to make sure that the default DRBD port 7780 is open on the firewall, and then you'll be ready to get going.

1. The name of the default DRBD configuration file is /etc/drbd.conf. This file serves as a starting point for finding the additional configuration, and to accomplish this goal, you'll have to include two lines that ensure that these configuration files can be found. To do this, make sure the following two lines are in the drbd.conf file:

    ```
    include "drbd.d/global_common.conf";
    include "drbd.d/*.res";
    ```

2. Now, you need to make sure that the real configuration is defined in the /etc/drbd.d/ global_common.conf file. Make sure it includes the following generic settings for smooth operation:

    ```
    global {
        minor-count  5;
        dialog-refresh       1;
    }
    common {
    }
    ```

3. For the next part of the configuration, you'll have to define the DRBD resource itself. This is done by creating several configuration files, one for each resource. Just make sure that this resource-specific configuration file is using the extension .res, to have it included in the configuration, as indicated in the /etc/drbd.conf file. Following, you can see what the configuration file would look like for a DRBD resource with the name drbd0. Note that the handlers section has to be present only if you're integrating DRBD with a Pacemaker cluster. Don't include it in setting up the initial synchronization on the DRBD! That's why, in the following listing, that part of the configuration is followed by hashes:

```
resource drbd0 {
   protocol      C;
   disk {
      on-io-error        pass_on;
    #  fencing resource-only;
   }
   #handlers {
   #    fence-peer "/usr/lib/drbd/crm-fence-peer.sh";
   #    after-resync-target "/usr/lib/drbd/crm-unfence-peer.sh";
   #}
   on node2 {
      disk      /dev/vdb;
      device    /dev/drbd0;
      address   192.168.122.131:7676;
      meta-disk internal;
   }
   on node1 {
      disk      /dev/vdb;
      device    /dev/drbd0;
      address   192.168.122.130:7676;
      meta-disk internal;
   }
   syncer {
      rate 7M;
   }
}
```

As the first part of this file, the name of the resource is defined. In this case, we're using drbd0, but you're completely free to choose any name you like. Next, the name of the device node, as it will occur in the /dev directory, is specified, including the minor number that is used for this device. Make sure that you select a unique resource name, as well as device name; otherwise, the kernel won't be able to distinguish between different DRBDs that you might be using.

Next, you'll specify which local device is going to be replicated between nodes. Typically, this is an empty device, but it is possible to put a device with an existing file system on it in a DRBD configuration and synchronize the contents of that file system to the other device in the DRBD pair. Following the name of the device, you'll include the configuration for the different nodes. The node names must be equal to the kernel names as returned by the uname command. As the last part, you'll set the synchronization speed. This determines the amount of bandwidth that is available for DRBD. Don't set this too high, if you don't have a dedicated network connection for DRBD; otherwise, you might be using all the bandwidth, and you'll risk other traffic not being able to get through, which may result in cluster nodes being STONITHed.

4. After creating the initial configuration files on one node, it's a good idea to verify the configuration. To do this, use the command drbdadm dump all. If this command displays the contents of all the configuration files (instead of complaining about missing parts of the configuration), everything is okay, and you can proceed to the next step.

5. After verifying the configuration on the first node, you can transfer it to the second node. Make sure that you can perform the transfer using the node name of the other node. If nodes cannot reach each other by node name, your DRBD is going to fail. So, if necessary, configure your /etc/hosts or DNS before moving on.

    ```
    scp /etc/drbd.conf node2:/etc/
    scp /etc/drbd.d/* node2:/etc/drbd.d/
    ```

6. Now it's time to create the DRBD metadata on both nodes. First, use the drbdadm command as in the following example. Next, you can start the DRBD service, as follows:

    ```
    #drbdadm -- --ignore-sanity-checks create-md drbd0
    Writing meta data...
    initializing activity log
    NOT initialized bitmap
    New drbd meta data block successfully created.
    #service drbd start
    ```

At this point, you can start the DRBD service, using service drbd start. Next, request its status, using service drbd status. You'll then see that both devices have their status connected but also that both are set as secondary devices and that they're inconsistent.

```
node1:~ # service drbd status
drbd driver loaded OK; device status:
version: 8.4.1 (api:1/proto:86-100)
GIT-hash: 91b4c048c1a0e06777b5f65d312b38d47abaea80 build by phil@fat-tyre, 2011-12-20 12:43:15
m:res     cs         ro                   ds                      p  mounted  fstype
0:drbd0   Connected  Secondary/Secondary  Inconsistent/Inconsistent  C
```

7. Now you can start the synchronization on one of the nodes, using the following command:

    ```
    drbdadm -- --overwrite-data-of-peer primary drbd0
    ```

If you now use the service drbd status command again to monitor the current synchronization status, you'll see that the status is now set to synchronized (sync'ed) and that you have established a Primary/Secondary relationship. You'll now have to wait until the status on both nodes is UpToDate.

```
node1:~ # service drbd status
drbd driver loaded OK; device status:
version: 8.4.1 (api:1/proto:86-100)
GIT-hash: 91b4c048c1a0e06777b5f65d312b38d47abaea80 build by phil@fat-tyre, 2011-12-20 12:43:15
m:res     cs          ro                ds                    p  mounted  fstype
0:drbd0   SyncTarget  Secondary/Primary  Inconsistent/UpToDate  C
...       sync'ed:    4.3%              (1006992/1048508)K
```

When synchronization has completed, the output of the service drbd status command will look as following:

```
node1:~ # service drbd status
drbd driver loaded OK; device status:
version: 8.4.1 (api:1/proto:86-100)
GIT-hash: 91b4c048c1a0e06777b5f65d312b38d47abaea80 build by phil@fat-tyre, 2011-12-20 12:43:15
m:res   cs          ro                  ds                  p mounted fstype
0:drbd0 Connected   Secondary/Primary   UpToDate/UpToDate   C
```

Working with the DRBD

Once the devices have been fully synchronized (depending on the size of the devices, this can take a long time!), you can create a file system on the primary DRBD node. To do this, you can use the following commands:

```
mkfs.ext3 /dev/drbd0
mount /dev/drbd0 /mnt
```

If all goes well, the device will now be mounted on the primary node on the directory /mnt. If you now create files in that directory, they will immediately be synchronized to the other node. Because you are using a Primary/Secondary setup, however, it's not possible to access these files directly on the other node, but they are present, in case anything goes wrong.

If all was successful until now, you can perform a test in which you'll make the other node primary. To do this, use the following procedure:

1. Unmount the DRBD on node node1.

2. Use the following command to make node node1 the secondary: drbdadm secondary drbd0.

3. Now go to node node2 and promote the DRBD to primary, using the command drbdadm primary drbd0.

4. On node node2, use the command service drbd status to verify that all went well. If this is the case, your DRBD is now fully operational, and it's time to move on to the next step and integrate it in Pacemaker.

Troubleshooting the Disconnect State

If after a change of status, both nodes in the DRBD setup return to a StandAlone state, your DRBD setup is in a split-brain situation, where there is no way to verify which node contains the primary data set. To remedy such a situation, you must manually intervene, by selecting one node whose modifications will be discarded. (This node is referred to as the *split-brain victim*.) This intervention is performed using the following commands:

```
drbdadm secondary resource
drbdadm -- --discard-my-data connect resource
```

On the other node (the *split-brain survivor*), if its connection state is also StandAlone, you would enter the following:

```
drbdadm connect resource
```

Working with Dual Primary Mode

In some cases, it makes sense to configure DRBD for active/active mode, for instance, if you want to configure a platform for hosting KVM or Xen virtual machines, in which two hosts are used in a `fail-over` configuration, to allow all virtual machines on one host, if required. Note that in such a configuration, it is not necessary to manage the DRBD resources from the cluster. That is because no state management is required, as the only state the nodes are supposed to be in is `Primary` anyway.

To use an `active-active` configuration, you have to enter some additional configuration. First, in the resource definition, you'll have to include a net section that allows the use of two primaries and sets the correct synchronization protocol. Also, you'll require a startup section that automatically switches to the primary role on both nodes on startup. The following lines will do this for you:

```
resource drbd0
       net {
               protocol C;
               allow-two-primaries yes;
       }
       startup {
               become-primary-on-both;
       }
       ...
}
```

Integrating DRBD in Pacemaker Clusters

Using the `drbdadm` command, you can manually determine which node is going to be primary and which will be the secondary. In a real HA environment, you'll have to integrate the DRBD in the Pacemaker cluster software. Doing this assumes that the cluster will manage DRBD, and not the local administrator.

Before adding the resources to the cluster, you'll have to take some precautionary measures in the `drbd` resource file as well. By including the following lines, you'll make sure that if the DRBD replication link becomes disconnected, the `crm-fence-peer.sh` script contacts the cluster manager and determines the Pacemaker `master-slave` resource that is associated with this DRBD resource. Next, it will ensure that the `master-slave` resource in Pacemaker will no longer get promoted on any other node than the currently active one. This guarantees that you don't get in a situation in which you have two nodes both thinking that they're master, which will lead to a split-brain situation. To accomplish this, include the following in the resource configuration file:

```
resource drbd0 {
       disk {
               fencing resource-only;
               ...
       }
       handlers {
               fence-peer "/usr/lib/drbd/crm-fence-peer.sh";
               after-resync-target "/usr/lib/drbd/crm-unfence-peer.sh";
       ...
       }
       ...
}
```

The next steps describe how to add a resource that manages DRBD in Pacemaker. This procedure assumes that you already have an operational Pacemaker cluster.

1. Start Hawk and log in as user hacluster.

2. Add a primitive for the DRBD resource. Select class OCF, the Provider Linbit, and the type drbd.

3. Set the drbd_resource parameter to the name of the drbd resource that you've created. This is the name of the resource as defined in the drbd0.res file and not the name of the device, so enter drbd0 and not /dev/drbd0.

4. From the parameters drop-down list, select the drbdconf parameter and provide the value of the drbd.conf file, which would be /etc/drbd.conf. Also, add the resource name, which should be the same as the name of the resource as defined in the DRBD resource file. Next, click Create Resource, to add the resource to your configuration.

5. At this point, go back to the resources tab and add a master-slave resource. Give it the name drbd-ms, and as the child resource, select the drbd resource you've just created.

6. Under Meta-Attributes, set the target role to Started and click Create Master/Slave to add the master-slave resource to the configuration.

```
primitive drbd ocf:linbit:drbd \
        params drbdconf="/etc/drbd.conf" drbd_resource="drbd0" \
        op start interval="0" timeout="240" \
        op monitor interval="20" role="Slave" timeout="20" start-delay="60" \
        op monitor interval="10" role="Master" timeout="20" start-delay="60"\
        op stop interval="0" timeout="100" \
        meta target-role="Started"
ms drbd-ms drbd \
            meta master-max="1" master-node-max="1" clone-max="2" \
            clone-node-max="1" notify="true" \
        meta target-role="Started"
```

Testing

Before you continue using your setup and add the iSCSI target to the configuration, it's a good idea to reboot both nodes in the cluster and make sure that the cluster is indeed managing the DRBD resource and not the local DRBD service. After the restart, verify that the DRBD resource is started on both nodes, where one of the nodes is used as the primary and the other is secondary. It's also a good idea to check the cluster configuration itself. As this is a two-node cluster, make sure the no-quorum policy is set to ignore. Also, make sure that STONITH is operational. If this is the case, you can perform a test and switch off the primary node. The secondary node should now automatically take over.

Adding an iSCSI Target to the Open Source SAN

Once your DRBD is operational and managed by the cluster, you have to add an iSCSI target to it. In Chapter 2, you read how to set up storage, and the iSCSI target in particular. In this section, you'll read how to set up the iSCSI target to provide access to the active DRBD and have it managed by the cluster.

There are different approaches to set this up. Using a simplified architecture, you can set up a DRBD on top of shared storage (as described in the previous section). On top of that, you can configure an iSCSI target and a dedicated IP address. Figure 9-1 provides an overview of this configuration. Even if this option works, it won't offer you much flexibility at the storage layer, because you will need a new DRBD for every additional iSCSI LUN that will be added. This is fine, if you're not anticipating many changes, but if you do expect changes in the storage topology, you might prefer a configuration that is more flexible.

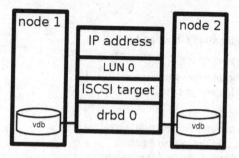

Figure 9-1. *Open source SAN simple configuration*

That is why it is much more flexible to create the LVM layer on top of the DRBD. This allows you to be flexible with regard to the sizes of the LUNs you're offering to the iSCSI initiators. Figure 9-2 gives an overview of this configuration.

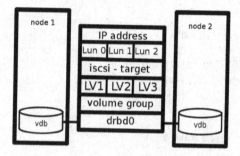

Figure 9-2. *Open source SAN complex configuration*

In the complex configuration, lots of components are required to work together, including the following:

1. A DRBD

2. The DRBD master that is managed from the cluster

3. An LVM configuration with a physical volume (PV), volume group (VG), and logical volume (LV)on top of the DRBD

4. An iSCSI target

5. An iSCSI logical unit that replaces the definition of the LUN in the iSCSI target configuration file

6. An IP address that allows nodes to connect to the configuration.

In the preceding section, you learned how to set up the DRBD and the DRBD master in a cluster environment. In Chapter 2, you learned how to set up an iSCSI. In this section, you read how to set up a clusterized iSCSI target and iSCSI logical unit, and an IP address on top of that. You will also learn how to set up the LVM configuration in a way that works in clustered environments.

Creating an Open Source SAN with LVM

To start with, you need to create an LVM physical volume on top of the DRBD. Access to the LVM volume group has to be set up as managed by the cluster next. To create this configuration, take the following steps:

1. Make sure that the DRBD is scanned by LVM for LVM metadata. To do this, you have to change the contents of the /etc/lvm/lvm.conf file to include the DRBDs. This following example will only consider DRBDs and ignore everything else:

   ```
   filter = [ "a|/dev/drbd.*|", "r|.*|" ]
   ```

2. Now you have to disable the LVM cache on both nodes. Do this by including the following line, also in /etc/lvm/lvm.conf:

   ```
   write_cache_state = 0
   ```

Always make sure to remove the current cache that might be existing: rm -rf /etc/lvm/.cache.

3. Before continuing, use the command vgscan to update LVM metadata.

4. Assuming the name of the DRBD is drbd0, use pvcreate /dev/drbd0 to mark the DRBD as a physical volume.

5. Now you can create the LVM stack, consisting of a PV, a VG, and an LV. The following three commands will create the volume group and a 1GB logical volume as well. Issue them on the node that currently has the primary DRBD device (!):

   ```
   pvcreate /dev/drbd0
   vgcreate vgdrbd /dev/drbd/by-res/drbd0
   lvcreate -L 1G -n lvlun0 vgdrbd
   ```

6. At this point, you can put the LVM configuration in the cluster. Type crm configure edit and add the following lines to the cluster configuration:

   ```
   primitive lvm-drbdvol ocf:heartbeat:LVM \
           params volgrpname="vgdrbd" \
           op monitor interval="10s" timeout="30s" depth="0"
   ```

7. Verify that the volume group resource is running in the cluster, before continuing.

Setting Up the iSCSI Target in the Cluster

Now that you've added the DRBD and LVM resources in the cluster, you can continue and configure iSCSI. What you need at this point is an iSCSI target. The configuration related to the iSCSI target consists of three different parts:

- The iSCSI target process that needs to be started by the cluster
- The iSCSILogicalUnit resource, which manages the LUNs that are presented by the iSCSI target
- A cluster IP address that will be used to access the iSCSI target

1. Make sure the iSCSI target software is installed on your computer. In Chapter 2, you can read in detail about all the different options that exist for creating an iSCSI target. In this procedure, I'll show you how to work with the tgt iSCSI target software that you may still encounter on older Linux distributions. Before proceeding, type { yum | zypper | install tgtd to install the software. Notice that this installs the tgt target software and not the ietd. The tgt software offers more advanced ways to define node restrictions, and therefore, I prefer it for complex environments.

2. Make sure that the iSCSI target software is not started automatically when your server boots, using either chkconfig tgtd off or sysctl disable tgtd.

3. Add the service to the cluster by using crm configure edit and include the following. (Note that you initially don't start the iSCSI target, because it needs additional configuration.)

    ```
    primitive iscsitarget-drbd ocf:heartbeat:iSCSITarget \
            params iqn="iqn.2014-02.com.example:drbdsan" tid="1" \
                    implementation="tgt" \
            op monitor interval="10s" timeout="20s" \
            meta target-role="Stopped"
    ```

4. At this point, you can add the iSCSI LUN, by adding a cluster resource. Note that on normal configurations, you would do this in the iSCSI configuration file, but you can do it perfectly from the cluster as well. The advantage is that the cluster will take care of making the required configuration present on all nodes in the cluster.

    ```
    primitive drbdvol-lun0 ocf:heartbeat:iSCSILogicalUnit \
            params target_iqn="iqn.2014-02.com.example:drbdsan" lun="1" \
            path="/dev/vgdrbd/lvlun0" \
            op monitor interval="10"
    ```

At this point, you can start the software in the cluster to begin using your iSCSI-based open source SAN. In the following sample configuration, you can see everything coming together. First, let's have a look at the cluster configuration.

```
chimay:~ # cat cluster-santnet-san.conf
node san-1.example.com
node san-2.example.com
primitive drbd_sandisk0 ocf:linbit:drbd \
        params drbd_resource="sandisk0" drbdconf="/etc/drbd.conf" \
        op stop interval="0" timeout="100" \
        op start interval="0" timeout="240" \
        op monitor interval="20" role="Slave" timeout="20" start-delay="60" \
        op monitor interval="10" role="Master" timeout="20" start-delay="60"
primitive ip-iscsi ocf:heartbeat:IPaddr2 \
        params ip="172.16.50.20" cidr_netmask="24" \
        op stop interval="0" timeout="20s" \
        op monitor interval="10s" timeout="20s" \
        op start interval="0" timeout="20s"
```

```
primitive iscsitarget lsb:iscsitarget \
        op stop interval="0" timeout="15" \
        op start interval="0" timeout="15" \
        op monitor interval="15" timeout="15"
primitive vgsan ocf:heartbeat:LVM \
        params volgrpname="vgsan" \
        op monitor interval="10s" timeout="30" depth="0"
group iscsi-group vgsan ip-iscsi iscsitarget \
        meta target-role="Started"
ms sandisk_ms drbd_sandisk0 \
        meta clone-max="2" target-role="Started" notify="true"
order vgsan-after-drbd 1000: sandisk_ms iscsi-group
property $id="cib-bootstrap-options" \
        dc-version="1.1.6-b988976485d15cb702c9307df55512d323831a5e" \
        cluster-infrastructure="openais" \
        no-quorum-policy="ignore" \
        stonith-enabled="false" \
        expected-quorum-votes="2" \
        last-lrm-refresh="1393398237"
```

You can see that the essence of this configuration consists of two parts: the DRBD that is managed with the master-slave resource drbd and the iscsi-group that is started after that device and makes sure that the iSCSI target is available at a fixed IP address.

In this cluster, the ietd iSCSI target was used, because it's an easy setup. The configuration in /etc/ietd.conf looks as follows:

```
Target iqn.2014-02.santnet.sante:target1
Lun 0 Path=/dev/vgsan/lun0,Type=fileio
Lun 1 Path=/dev/vgsan/lun1,Type=fileio
Lun 2 Path=/dev/vgsan/lun2,Type=fileio
Lun 3 Path=/dev/vgsan/lun3,Type=fileio
```

The configuration of the DRBD is very similar to the configuration described previously in this chapter.

```
san-1:/etc/drbd.d # cat sandisk0.res
resource sandisk0 {
        protocol        C;
        disk {
                on-io-error     pass_on;
                fencing resource-only;
        }
        handlers {
                fence-peer "/usr/lib/drbd/crm-fence-peer.sh";
                after-resync-target "/usr/lib/drbd/crm-unfence-peer.sh";
        }
        on san-2.example.com {
                disk      /dev/sdb;
                device    /dev/drbd0;
                address      172.17.50.22:7676;
                meta-disk internal;
        }
```

```
on san-1.example.com {
        disk         /dev/sdb;
        device /dev/drbd0;
        address 172.17.50.21:7676;
        meta-disk internal;
}
syncer {
        rate 70M;
}
}
```

Behind the drbd0 iSCSI device is a 1.5TB disk device, servicing dozens of iSCSI initiator hosts in a highly commercial environment.

Summary

In this chapter, you have learned how to configure an open source storage area network (SAN), using Pacemaker and other open source software. The result is a serious SAN that can be used in production environments and that is actually operational at different customers' sites around the globe. In Chapter 10, you will learn about another use case, in which Pacemaker is used to provide high availability services for KVM or Xen virtual machines.

■ ■ ■

Use Case: Creating a Solution for Xen/KVM High Availability

In previous chapters, you read how virtual machines were used as cluster nodes, to ensure that availability of vital resources is maximized. But what happens if the virtual machine itself goes down? Chances are that you're using VMware and, within VMware, have configured high availability (HA), which ensures that the virtual machines themselves are restarted, if they go down. In this chapter, you'll learn how to create an alternative, using open source software.

In this chapter, the following topics are covered:

- Open source virtualization solutions

- Requirements for setting up an HA solution for virtual machines

- Example of a virtual machine HA cluster

- Configuration of Xen virtual machines

- Configuration of KVMs (Kernal-based Virtual Machines)

Introduction: An Overview of Open Source Virtualization Solutions

VMware is dominating the market of virtualization solutions. But using VMware doesn't make sense, if all you're running is Linux servers. Within Linux, there are different excellent solutions for virtualization: KVM, Xen, and Linux containers. The advantage of all of these is that the technique is included in modern Linux distributions, so the solution is available for free.

Xen

Of the three leading Linux virtualization solutions, Xen is the oldest. It became popular around the year 2006, by introducing some solutions that were never seen before in the world of virtualization, and the Xen hypervisor was included with leading Linux distributions, such as SUSE and Red Hat.

From the beginning, Xen had a hard time getting adopted by the Linux kernel. Many patches were applied to the Linux kernel to make Xen virtualization happen, and that was the main reason why Xen didn't become very popular in the community of Linux developers. The popularity of the Xen project decreased even more when the company that was created by the founders of Xen was acquired by Citrix, which made the future of Xen as an open source virtualization platform even more uncertain.

Citrix, however, wasn't really capable of turning Xen into a major success, which has led to the company largely abandoning Xen virtualization, as well as its XenServer, the commercial solution that is based on Xen. As a result of these events, it became possible for the Linux Foundation to take over the Xen project, which led to a revival of Xen in the year 2013.

For some Linux distributions, Xen is still an important solution. SUSE and Oracle Linux are offering virtualization solutions that are based on Xen, and with good reason, as some important customers have adopted Xen as their default virtualization solution. There's a reason why they've done that. Xen has been around for a long time now, and the solution is stable. With the Linux Foundation taking over Xen, and important enterprise distributions such as the SUSE Linux Enterprise Server, that are still offering Xen support, Xen for sure has a bright future.

KVM

Kernal-based Virtual Machine (KVM) *is* Linux kernel virtualization. The big advantage of KVM is that it is simple: every Linux kernel includes the two kernel modules that are required for setting up a KVM virtual environment. To use KVM virtualization, you need hardware support for virtualization on the CPU of your server. This support is offered by default on most server-grade CPUs, but on the more basic CPU models, it may be missing, which makes it impossible to use KVM virtualization.

KVM has become the leading hypervisor-based virtualization solution on Linux, especially since Red Hat adopted the solution as its default and only virtualization solution, with the launch of Red Hat Enterprise Linux 6.

Requirements for Setting Up an HA Solution for Virtual Machines

For setting up a virtual machine cluster, a few specific items have to be set up. First and foremost, you need a solution that allows multiple host computers to access the virtual machines simultaneously. In most cases, this is accomplished by putting the virtual machine image files on a storage area network (SAN). Next, the hosts need a connection to the SAN that allows them to access the virtual machine files and to write to the virtual machine files simultaneously. There are three possible solutions.

- You can set up a cluster file system such as GFS2 or OCFS2. This solution makes sense, if you want to configure the virtual machines with an image file rather than a raw storage device that is used for access.

- You can set up a clustered LVM volume group with a logical volume that is accessible by all nodes simultaneously. This setup allows for a configuration in which the virtual machine uses a storage device as the back end for its virtual disk, which offers a somewhat more robust and faster configuration.

- You can arrange simultaneous access through a file-sharing service, such as NFS. This is the least preferable solution, because file access via an NFS server is slower than direct file access, and you would also need to take care of setting up a high availability solution for the NFS server itself.

In theory, you could also set up a virtualization cluster on top of storage that can be accessed by one node at the same time only.

Example of a Virtual Machine HA Cluster

There are different ways of creating a cluster for Xen virtual machines. The example from Listing 10-1 is used in practice to guarantee the availability of Xen virtual machines.

Listing 10-1. Xen HA Cluster

```
node xen-ha-01 \
        attributes standby="off"
node xen-ha-02 \
        attributes standby="off"
node xen-ha-03 \
        attributes standby="off"
node xen-ha-04 \
        attributes standby="off"
primitive clvmd ocf:lvm2:clvmd \
        operations $id="clvmd-operations" \
        op monitor interval="10" timeout="20" \
        op start interval="0" timeout="90" \
        op stop interval="0" timeout="100" \
        params daemon_timeout="80"
primitive controld ocf:pacemaker:controld \
        operations $id="controld-operations" \
        op monitor interval="10" timeout="20" start-delay="0" \
        op start interval="0" timeout="90" \
        op stop interval="0" timeout="100"
primitive fs_shared-fs ocf:heartbeat:Filesystem \
        operations $id="fs_shared-fs-operations" \
        op monitor interval="20" timeout="40" \
        op start interval="0" timeout="60" \
        op stop interval="0" timeout="60" \
        op notify interval="0" timeout="60" \
        params device="/dev/shared-fs/shared-fsvol" directory="/shared-fs" fstype="ocfs2"
primitive lvm_activate ocf:heartbeat:LVM \
        operations $id="lvm_activate-operations" \
        op monitor interval="10" timeout="180" \
        op start interval="0" timeout="120" \
        op stop interval="0" timeout="120" \
        params volgrpname="shared-fs" exclusive="false" partial_activation="true"
primitive o2cb ocf:ocfs2:o2cb \
        operations $id="o2cb-operations" \
        op monitor interval="10" timeout="20" \
        op start interval="0" timeout="90" \
        op stop interval="0" timeout="100"
primitive ping ocf:pacemaker:ping \
        operations $id="ping-operations" \
        op monitor interval="10" timeout="60" \
        op start interval="0" timeout="60" \
        params host_list="192.168.1.254" multiplier="1000"
primitive stonith_sbd stonith:external/sbd \
        meta target-role="Started" \
        operations $id="stonith_sbd-operations" \
        op monitor interval="15" timeout="120" start-delay="15"
```

```
primitive xend lsb:xend \
        operations $id="xend-operations" \
        op monitor interval="15" timeout="30" \
        op start interval="0" timeout="300" \
        op stop interval="0" timeout="300"
primitive xen-vm-01 ocf:heartbeat:Xen \
        meta target-role="Started" allow-migrate="true" \
        operations $id="xen-vm-01-operations" \
        op start interval="0" timeout="5400" \
        op stop interval="0" timeout="5400" \
        op monitor interval="300" timeout="300" start-delay="600" \
        op migrate_to interval="0" timeout="3600" \
        op migrate_from interval="0" timeout="120" \
        params xmfile="/shared-fs/xen-ha/configs/xen-vm-01.cfg"
primitive xen-vm-02 ocf:heartbeat:Xen \
        meta target-role="Started" allow-migrate="true" \
        operations $id="xen-vm-02-operations" \
        op start interval="0" timeout="5400" \
        op stop interval="0" timeout="5400" \
        op monitor interval="300" timeout="300" start-delay="600" \
        op migrate_to interval="0" timeout="3600" \
        op migrate_from interval="0" timeout="120" \
        params xmfile="/shared-fs/xen-ha/configs/xen-vm-02.cfg"
primitive xen-vm-03 ocf:heartbeat:Xen \
        meta target-role="Started" allow-migrate="true" \
        operations $id="xen-vm-03-operations" \
        op start interval="0" timeout="5400" \
        op stop interval="0" timeout="5400" \
        op monitor interval="300" timeout="300" start-delay="600" \
        op migrate_to interval="0" timeout="3600" \
        op migrate_from interval="0" timeout="120" \
        params xmfile="/shared-fs/xen-ha/configs/xen-vm-03.cfg"
primitive xen-vm-04 ocf:heartbeat:Xen \
        meta allow-migrate="true" target-role="Started" \
        operations $id="xen-vm-04-operations" \
        op start interval="0" timeout="5400" \
        op stop interval="0" timeout="5400" \
        op monitor interval="300" timeout="300" start-delay="600" \
        op migrate_to interval="0" timeout="3600" \
        op migrate_from interval="0" timeout="120" \
        params xmfile="/shared-fs/xen-ha/configs/xen-vm-04.cfg"
primitive xen-vm-05 ocf:heartbeat:Xen \
        meta target-role="Started" allow-migrate="true" \
        operations $id="xen-vm-05-operations" \
        op start interval="0" timeout="5400" \
        op stop interval="0" timeout="5400" \
        op monitor interval="300" timeout="300" start-delay="600" \
        op migrate_to interval="0" timeout="3600" \
        op migrate_from interval="0" timeout="120" \
        params xmfile="/shared-fs/xen-ha/configs/xen-vm-05.cfg"
```

```
primitive xen-vm-06 ocf:heartbeat:Xen \
        meta target-role="Started" allow-migrate="true" \
        operations $id="xen-vm-06-operations" \
        op start interval="0" timeout="5400" \
        op stop interval="0" timeout="5400" \
        op monitor interval="300" timeout="300" start-delay="600" \
        op migrate_to interval="0" timeout="3600" \
        op migrate_from interval="0" timeout="120" \
        params xmfile="/shared-fs/xen-ha/configs/xen-vm-06.cfg"
primitive xen-vm-07 ocf:heartbeat:Xen \
        meta target-role="Started" allow-migrate="true" \
        operations $id="xen-vm-07-operations" \
        op start interval="0" timeout="5400" \
        op stop interval="0" timeout="5400" \
        op monitor interval="300" timeout="300" start-delay="600" \
        op migrate_to interval="0" timeout="3600" \
        op migrate_from interval="0" timeout="120" \
        params xmfile="/shared-fs/xen-ha/configs/xen-vm-07.cfg"
primitive xen-vm-08 ocf:heartbeat:Xen \
        meta target-role="Started" allow-migrate="true" \
        operations $id="xen-vm-08-operations" \
        op start interval="0" timeout="5400" \
        op stop interval="0" timeout="5400" \
        op monitor interval="300" timeout="300" start-delay="600" \
        op migrate_to interval="0" timeout="3600" \
        op migrate_from interval="0" timeout="120" \
        params xmfile="/shared-fs/xen-ha/configs/xen-vm-08.cfg"
primitive xen-vm-09 ocf:heartbeat:Xen \
        meta target-role="Started" allow-migrate="true" \
        operations $id="xen-vm-09-operations" \
        op start interval="0" timeout="5400" \
        op stop interval="0" timeout="5400" \
        op monitor interval="300" timeout="300" start-delay="600" \
        op migrate_to interval="0" timeout="3600" \
        op migrate_from interval="0" timeout="120" \
        params xmfile="/shared-fs/xen-ha/configs/xen-vm-09.cfg"
group storage_group controld clvmd o2cb lvm_activate fs_shared-fs
clone ping_clone ping \
        meta target-role="Started" ordered="true"
clone storage_clone storage_group \
        meta target-role="Started" ordered="true"
clone xend_clone xend \
        meta target-role="Started" ordered="true"
location location_xen-vm-01 xen-vm-01 100: xen-ha-01
location location_xen-vm-02 xen-vm-02 100: xen-ha-01
location location_xen-vm-03 xen-vm-03 100: xen-ha-01
location location_xen-vm-04 xen-vm-04 100: xen-ha-02
location location_xen-vm-05 xen-vm-05 100: xen-ha-02
location location_xen-vm-06 xen-vm-06 100: xen-ha-03
location location_xen-vm-07 xen-vm-07 100: xen-ha-03
location location_xen-vm-08 xen-vm-08 100: xen-ha-04
location location_xen-vm-09 xen-vm-09 100: xen-ha-04
```

```
location ping_xen-vm-01 xen-vm-01 \
        rule $id="ping_xen-vm-01-rule" -inf: pingd lte 0
location ping_xen-vm-02 xen-vm-02 \
        rule $id="ping_xen-vm-02-rule" -inf: pingd lte 0
location ping_xen-vm-03 xen-vm-03 \
        rule $id="ping_xen-vm-03-rule" -inf: pingd lte 0
location ping_xen-vm-04 xen-vm-04 \
        rule $id="ping_xen-vm-04-rule" -inf: pingd lte 0
location ping_xen-vm-05 xen-vm-05 \
        rule $id="ping_xen-vm-05-rule" -inf: pingd lte 0
location ping_xen-vm-06 xen-vm-06 \
        rule $id="ping_xen-vm-06-rule" -inf: pingd lte 0
location ping_xen-vm-07 xen-vm-07 \
        rule $id="ping_xen-vm-07-rule" -inf: pingd lte 0
location ping_xen-vm-08 xen-vm-08 \
        rule $id="ping_xen-vm-08-rule" -inf: pingd lte 0
location ping_xen-vm-09 xen-vm-09 \
        rule $id="ping_xen-vm-09-rule" -inf: pingd lte 0
colocation storage_clone-with-xend_clone inf: storage_clone xend_clone
colocation xend_clone-with-ping_clone inf: xend_clone ping_clone
order storage_clone-after-xend_clone 0: xend_clone storage_clone
order xend_clone-after-ping_clone 0: ping_clone xend_clone
order xen-vm-01-after-storage_clone 0: storage_clone xen-vm-01
order xen-vm-02-after-storage_clone 0: storage_clone xen-vm-02
order xen-vm-03-after-storage_clone 0: storage_clone xen-vm-03
order xen-vm-04-after-storage_clone 0: storage_clone xen-vm-04
order xen-vm-05-after-storage_clone 0: storage_clone xen-vm-05
order xen-vm-06-after-storage_clone 0: storage_clone xen-vm-06
order xen-vm-07-after-storage_clone 0: storage_clone xen-vm-07
order xen-vm-08-after-storage_clone 0: storage_clone xen-vm-08
order xen-vm-09-after-storage_clone 0: storage_clone xen-vm-09
property $id="cib-bootstrap-options" \
        dc-version="1.1.7-77eeb099a504ceda05d648ed161ef8b1582c7daf" \
        cluster-infrastructure="openais" \
        expected-quorum-votes="4" \
        no-quorum-policy="ignore" \
        stonith-action="poweroff" \
        default-resource-stickiness="INFINITY" \
        stonith-enabled="true" \
        symmetric-cluster="true" \
        stonith-timeout="60s" \
        maintenance-mode="false" \
        last-lrm-refresh="1384353701"
```

This configuration is used for a four-node cluster in which resources for an OCFS2 shared file system on top of cLVM logical volumes is used. In this configuration, you can see the use of some resource agents and parameters that haven't been discussed before.

First, there is the ping resource.

```
primitive ping ocf:pacemaker:ping \
        operations $id="ping-operations" \
        op monitor interval="10" timeout="60" \
        op start interval="0" timeout="60" \
        params host_list="192.168.1.254" multiplier="1000"
```

This resource is used as a helper resource that monitors whether the node is still connected to the network. The ping resource periodically pings a node that is supposed to be available at all times, in this case, the default gateway. The secret of this resource is that it is used in a constraint, which creates a dependency between the ping resource and the other resource(s) in the constraint. In this configuration, if the ping resource fails its test and generates an exit code 0, it will fail the depending resource on that node as well, thus forcing a migration of the resource to another node. When using a ping resource, make sure at all times to use the parameter multiplier=1000, or else it won't work. Note that the ping resource is configured as a clone, which ensures that it is started on all hosts in the cluster.

For the virtual machines themselves, two primitives are used (see Listing 10-2). First, there is the xend primitive. xend is the interface that is required for managing Xen virtual machines, and it must be available before any virtual machine is started. xend is a relatively simple resource, which is why the resource is configured as an LSB resource. Next, the Xen virtual machines are defined.

Listing 10-2. Required Resources for the Xen HA

```
primitive xend lsb:xend \
        operations $id="xend-operations" \
        op monitor interval="15" timeout="30" \
        op start interval="0" timeout="300" \
        op stop interval="0" timeout="300"
primitive xen-vm-01 ocf:heartbeat:Xen \
        meta target-role="Started" allow-migrate="true" \
        operations $id="xen-vm-01-operations" \
        op start interval="0" timeout="5400" \
        op stop interval="0" timeout="5400" \
        op monitor interval="300" timeout="300" start-delay="600" \
        op migrate_to interval="0" timeout="3600" \
        op migrate_from interval="0" timeout="120" \
        params xmfile="/shared-fs/xen-ha/configs/xen-vm-01.cfg"
```

The OCF resources for Xen virtual machines have a few specific attributes. First, they require the meta attribute allow-migrate="true". This parameter is required to allow for live migration. Also, notice that the Xen RA has a migrate to and a migrate from parameter, which defines the time-outs for a migration away from the current location and a migration to the current location. Next, there is the xmfile parameter, which specifies where the configuration file for the Xen virtual machine can be found.

Because it makes sense that all the virtual machines are started at a preferred node, there are a couple of location constraints, each with a score of 100. This expresses a slight preference for the resources to run each on its preferred node.

Last, there are the generic cluster properties. An interesting parameter is the no-quorum-policy, which is set to ignore. That means that in case quorum is lost, the resources can still be migrated to the remaining nodes. The idea behind this is that two nodes should suffice to run all virtual machines, and STONITH in this cluster is set up in a way that guarantees that a split-brain situation can never occur. Also, notice default-resource-stickiness, which is set to INFINITY. This ensures that the resources will stay where they are and never be migrated automatically, which would be very bad for the availability of the services.

Creating a KVM HA Cluster

Many small environments are using KVM for high availability—not KVM in a managed solution like oVirt, but plain KVM, where virtual machines are running directly on top of the hypervisor that is integrated in the Linux operating system. In too many cases, it's just KVM, and no measures have been taken to make sure that business goes on if the host goes down. In this section, you'll read how to provide a simple solution that takes care of ensuring the availability of KVM virtual machines.

KVM is offered with the Linux kernel, so you can use it on any Linux distribution (Figure 10-1). For the KVM part, there won't be many differences. For the clustering part, however, there will. Even if clustering is more or less the same on most Linux distributions, there are small differences that really do matter. As the Pacemaker stack originated from the SUSE distribution, and Red Hat is just finalizing its solution in recent versions, in this section, I prefer explaining the SUSE configuration. While trying to configure the setup described in this section on Red Hat, there are still some rough edges that take away the flexibility to configure the solution that fits your needs best. On SUSE, it all just works. The version used is a completely patched OpenSUSE 13.1.

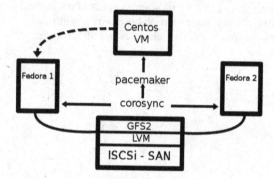

Figure 10-1. KVM virtualization overview

The procedure described here assumes that the nodes are already configured to a storage area network (SAN). If this is not the case, it is relatively easy to connect virtualization hosts to a Linux SAN, which is offered shared storage based on the LIO or IET iSCSI target. You can, of course, also use an SAN appliance, if your environment has one. Do make sure, though, that you're using an SAN and not network-attached storage (NAS). High availability based on NAS is possible for virtual machines but not recommended, for performance and reliability reasons. Also, in the following procedure, you'll learn how to build the cluster, using the OCFS2 shared file system, and that only works if you're on an SAN.

To configure a KVM HA cluster, the following steps must to be performed:

1. Create the base cluster.

2. Configure an OCFS2 cluster file system on the SAN.

3. Install a KVM virtual machine using the SAN disk as the storage back end.

4. Set up Pacemaker cluster resources for the KVM virtual machine.

5. Verify the cluster configuration.

Creating the Base Cluster

To create the basic cluster on OpenSUSE 13.1, you have to perform the following steps:

1. Use `zypper in pacemaker ocfs2-tools lvm2-clvm` to install all of the packages required to build the cluster.

2. The cluster consists of two layers. The lower layer takes care of communications in the cluster and is called Corosync. The upper layer takes care of resource management. To configure the lower layer, a good sample configuration file is provided with the name `/etc/corosync/corosync.conf.example`. Copy this file to the file `/etc/corosync/corosync.conf` and make sure to modify the following lines:

    ```
    bindnetaddr: 192.168.4.0

    quorum {
            # Enable and configure quorum subsystem (default: off)
            # see also corosync.conf.5 and votequorum.5
            provider: corosync_votequorum
            expected_votes: 2
    }
    ```

    The `bindnetaddr` line should reflect the IP network address that your node uses to communicate on the network. The quorum lines tell the cluster how many nodes to expect.

3. Start and enable the Corosync and Pacemaker services, using `systemctl start corosync; systemctl start pacemaker; systemctl enable corosync; systemctl enable pacemaker`.

4. Type `crm_mon`. This should give an output as in Listing 10-1, which verifies that the cluster is operational.

    ```
    Last updated: Sun May 11 19:38:24 2014
    Last change: Sun May 11 19:38:24 2014 by root via cibadmin on suse1
    Stack: corosync
    Current DC: suse1 (3232236745) - partition with quorum
    Version: 1.1.10-1.2-d9bb763
    2 Nodes configured
    0 Resources configured

    Online: [ suse1 suse2 ]
    ```

Configure the SAN for Shared Storage

To set up the OCFS2 shared file system, you first have to start some supporting services on the cluster. Type `crm configure edit` and make sure the following lines are added to the file:

```
primitive dlm ocf:pacemaker:controld \
        op start interval="0" timeout="90" \
        op stop interval="0" timeout="100" \
        op monitor interval="10" timeout="20" start-delay="0"
```

```
primitive o2cb ocf:ocfs2:o2cb \
        op stop interval="0" timeout="100" \
        op start interval="0" timeout="90" \
        op monitor interval="20" timeout="20"
group ocfs2-base-group dlm o2cb
clone ocfs2-base-clone ocfs2-base-group \
        meta ordered="true" clone-max="2" clone-node-max="1"
property $id="cib-bootstrap-options" \
        cluster-infrastructure="corosync" \
        stonith-enabled="false"
```

After starting these basic services, you can create the ocfs2 file system. To do this, type `mkfs.ocfs2 /dev/sdb`. Next, create a directory with the name /shared on both nodes and type `crm configure edit` again. At this point, add the following to the cluster configuration:

```
primitive ocfs-fs ocf:heartbeat:Filesystem \
        params fstype="ocfs2" device="/dev/disk/by-path/ip-192.168.1.125:3260-iscsi-iqn.2014-01.com.
example:kiabi" directory="/shared" \
        op stop interval="0" timeout="60" \
        op start interval="0" timeout="60" \
        op monitor interval="20" timeout="40"
clone ocfs-fs-clone ocfs-fs \
        meta clone-max="2" clone-node-max=1
order ocfs2-fs-after-ocfs-base 1000: ocfs2-base-clone ocfs-fs
```

Now, at both nodes, you should have a shared file system available and mounted on the /shared directory. Files that are written to one node will be immediately visible and accessible at the other node, which is exactly what you need to set up a high availability environment for virtual machines.

Installing a KVM Virtual Machine

To install KVM virtual machines, the virtualization host has to run the `libvirt` service. Use `systemctl start libvirtd; systemctl enable libvirtd` to do this. If this is the case, there are two solutions for starting the installation: you can either use the Virtual Machine Manager graphical tool, or you can use `virt-install`. The Virtual Machine Manager, which is started with the `virt-manager` command, requires an X-server to display its graphical windows and might, for that reason, not be feasible. The `virt-manager` utility is also useful, if no graphical environment is available, and allows you to create virtual machines from a scripted environment in a non-interactive way.

To start the VM installation using `virt-install`, you can use a command such as the following:

```
virt-install --name smallcent --ram 512 --disk path=/shared/smallcent.img,size=4 --network
network:default --vnc --cdrom /isos/CentOS-6.5-x86_64-bin-DVD1.iso
```

By this command, all properties of the virtual machine are specified. The name of the virtual machine is set to smallcent. This name is important, because it must be used when creating the cluster resource for the virtual machine. 512MB of RAM is allocated, and a disk file with a size of 4GB is created in the directory /shared. Note that this directory is supposed to be on the OCFS2 volume that was created in the previous step of this procedure.

For the network, a default configuration is used. The next parameter is important, because it opens a VNC viewer on the virtual machine, which allows the installation of the virtual machine to be completed interactively. The last parameter refers to the CD-ROM device that is used to complete the VM installation.

In this setup, an interactive installation is started. In some cases, this will not be feasible, because no terminal is connected to the virtualization host. In such a scenario, an automated installation has to be used. Covering such an installation goes beyond the scope of this book. Consult your distributions documentation for directions on how to set up an AutoYast (SUSE) or Kickstart (Red Hat) server that can help you with this.

Setting Up Cluster Resources for the KVM Virtual Machine

To integrate the virtual machine in the cluster, you have to make the configuration of the virtual machine available to the cluster. To do this, you have to dump the XML configuration of the virtual machine to a text file. First, use `virsh list --all` to verify the name of the virtual machine. In this example, the name of the virtual machine is `smallcent`. Because the cluster needs access to the XML file containing the definition of the virtual machine, you have to dump it to a file that is on the shared storage device that you've set up earlier. To do this, type `virsh dumpxml smallcent > /shared/smallcent.xml`.

At this point, you can create the resource for the virtual machine in the cluster. The `VirtualDomain` resource agent is used for this purpose. Use `crm configure edit` and include a configuration that looks like the following:

```
primitive smallcent ocf:pacemaker:VirtualDomain \
        params hypervisor="qemu:///system" migration_transport="ssh" config="/shared/smallcent.xml" \
        meta allow-migrate="true" \
        op stop timeout="120" interval="0" \
        op start timeout="120" interval="0" \
        op monitor interval="20" timeout="20"
```

Note that for the cluster to be able to manage the resource, it is essential that the XML file that contains the configuration be used from all nodes in the cluster. Therefore, you must make sure to put it on the shared storage device. In the preceding `pcs` command, you'll create a resource with the name `smallcent`, using the `VirtualDomain` resource agent. This resource agent must know where it can find the hypervisor, which is done by including `hypervisor="qemu://system"` in the resource definition. To allow for migration of this virtual machine, the `migration_transport` mechanism is defined as `ssh`. Note that this only works if the hosts are configured with keys that allow for automated login from one host to the other. Next, you have to indicate where the cluster can find the XML configuration that is used to manage the resource.

At this point, the configuration, as shown with `crm configure edit`, should resemble the following listing:

```
node $id="3232236745" suse1
node $id="3232236746" suse2
primitive dlm ocf:pacemaker:controld \
        op start interval="0" timeout="90" \
        op stop interval="0" timeout="100" \
        op monitor interval="10" timeout="20" start-delay="0"
primitive o2cb ocf:ocfs2:o2cb \
        op stop interval="0" timeout="100" \
        op start interval="0" timeout="90" \
        op monitor interval="20" timeout="20"
primitive smallcent ocf:pacemaker:VirtualDomain \
        params hypervisor="qemu:///system" migration_transport="ssh" config="/shared/smallcent.xml" \
        meta allow-migrate="true" \
        op stop timeout="120" interval="0" \
        op start timeout="120" interval="0" \
        op monitor interval="20" timeout="20"
```

```
group ocfs2-base-group dlm o2cb
clone ocfs2-base-clone ocfs2-base-group \
        meta ordered="true" clone-max="2" clone-node-max="1"
property $id="cib-bootstrap-options" \
        dc-version="1.1.10-1.2-d9bb763" \
        cluster-infrastructure="corosync" \
        stonith-enabled="false" \
        last-lrm-refresh="1399852426"
#vim:set syntax=pcmk
```

You can now verify the working of the configuration, using the crm_mon command. If all is configured correctly, you should now have a fully operational KVM high availability cluster.

Summary

In this chapter, you have learned how to set up a high availability cluster for virtual machines. The next and final chapter will show you how to set up a complex cluster where web servers and database servers that are both configured for high availability are working together.

■ ■ ■

## CHAPTER 11

Use Case: Configuring a Load-Balanced Mail Front End with a Database Back End

Customer Situation

The configuration that is described in this chapter is part of the most complex cluster that I have ever created. In fact, it's not just a cluster, it's a group of clusters working together to provide a highly redundant environment that is used by medical doctors in France to access a web-based mailbox. In this chapter, I'm only discussing a part of the configuration, in which two clusters are working together to deliver e-mail.

The customer expected a substantial workload, so it wanted an environment that is not only redundant from the perspective of high availability but that also offers simplified load-balancing services. The solution had to be portable and deployed at customer sites as an appliance; therefore, it had to contain everything from within, without any dependencies to external hardware or other resources. For that reason, the load balancing was taken care of by round-robin Domain Name System (DNS).

A challenge when working with round-robin DNS is that it is completely ignorant of the current state of the IP addresses in the round-robin configuration. In round-robin DNS, multiple IP addresses are configured for one DNS name. The first connection gets the first IP address, the second connection gets the second IP address, and so on. But if one of the IP addresses becomes unavailable, round-robin DNS will never know. Therefore, the cluster is configured with "floating" IP addresses on the public site of the cluster. These floating IP addresses ensure that all IP addresses that are configured in the round-robin DNS configuration will be available at all times, even if one of the servers goes down. This allows users to access the Postfix mail servers behind the IP addresses at all times.

At the back end, the customer was using an application that required access to a Postgres database. As the solution had to be highly available all the way, the Postgres database was in a cluster configuration as well. Note in the overview picture that the data this collection of clusters is accessing is on an open source SAN solution, as described in Chapter 9. Figure 11-1 gives an overview of the configuration.

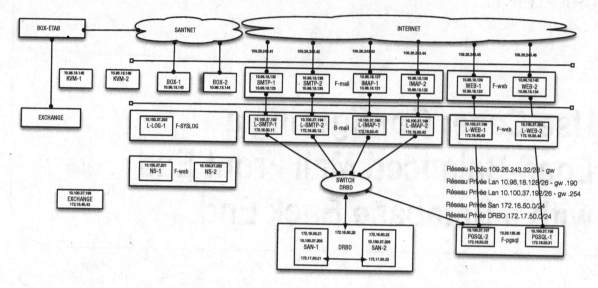

Figure 11-1. *Use case overview*

Database Back End

The back end of the cluster described in this chapter is the database. This cluster is relatively simple and runs on KVM virtual machines. Because KVM is used as the platform, the STONITH agents in this cluster are based on `libvirt`, as you can see in the sample code from Listing 11-1.

Listing 11-1. Database Cluster

```
chimay:~ # cat cluster-santnet-pgsql-new.conf
node pgsql-1.example.com
node pgsql-2.example.com
primitive db-pgsql ocf:heartbeat:pgsql \
        op stop interval="0" timeout="120" \
        op start interval="0" timeout="120" \
        op monitor interval="30" timeout="30" \
        meta target-role="Started"
primitive dlm ocf:pacemaker:controld \
        op start interval="0" timeout="90" \
        op stop interval="0" timeout="100" \
        op monitor interval="10" timeout="20" start-delay="0"
primitive ip-pgsql ocf:heartbeat:IPaddr2 \
        params cidr_netmask="24" ip="192.168.50.30" \
        op stop interval="0" timeout="20s" \
        op start interval="0" timeout="20s" \
        op monitor interval="10s" timeout="20s"
primitive o2cb ocf:ocfs2:o2cb \
        op stop interval="0" timeout="100" \
        op start interval="0" timeout="90" \
        op monitor interval="20" timeout="20"
```

```
primitive ocfs2-fs-pgsql ocf:heartbeat:Filesystem \
        params fstype="ocfs2" device="/dev/disk/by-path/ip-172.16.50.20:3260-iscsi-iqn.2014-02.
santnet.sante:target1-lun-0-part1" directory="/var/lib/pgsql" \
        op stop interval="0" timeout="60" \
        op start interval="0" timeout="60" \
        op monitor interval="20" timeout="40"
primitive stonith-vmkvm-pgsql-1 stonith:external/libvirt \
        params hostlist="pgsql-1" hypervisor_uri="qemu+ssh://chimay/system" \
        op monitor interval="60" timeout="20" start-delay="15" \
        op stop interval="0" timeout="15" \
        op start interval="0" timeout="20" \
        meta target-role="Started"
primitive stonith-vmkvm-pgsql-2 stonith:external/libvirt \
        params hostlist="pgsql-2" hypervisor_uri="qemu+ssh://chimay/system" \
        op monitor interval="60" timeout="20" start-delay="15" \
        op stop interval="0" timeout="15" \
        op start interval="0" timeout="20" \
        meta target-role="Started"
group ocfs2-base-group dlm o2cb
group pgsql-group ip-pgsql db-pgsql \
        meta target-role="Started"
clone ocfs2-base-clone ocfs2-base-group \
        meta ordered="true" interleaved="true" clone-max="2" clone-node-max="1"
target-role="Started"
clone ocfs2-fs-clone ocfs2-fs-pgsql \
        meta target-role="Started"
location fence-pgsql-1 stonith-vmkvm-pgsql-1 -inf: pgsql-1.example.com
location fence-pgsql-2 stonith-vmkvm-pgsql-2 -inf: pgsql-2.example.com
order ocfs2-fs-pgsql-after-ocfs2-base 1000: ocfs2-base-clone ocfs2-fs-clone
property $id="cib-bootstrap-options" \
        dc-version="1.1.6-b988976485d15cb702c9307df55512d323831a5e" \
        cluster-infrastructure="openais" \
        expected-quorum-votes="2" \
        no-quorum-policy="ignore" \
        stonith-action="poweroff" \
        last-lrm-refresh="1393400151"
```

When setting up a database cluster, this can be an active/active setup, a master-slave setup, or an active/passive setup. You might be tempted to think the setup has to be active/active or master-slave, but this is not required in most cases.

active/active database configurations are required only in high-load environments. The same goes for master-slave configurations. Also, in nearly all cases, to create a master-slave configuration, support in the database itself is required. This support, in most cases, also means that additional licenses have to be purchased, and that makes master-slave configurations in general relatively expensive.

The main difference between a master-slave database configuration and an active/passive configuration is that in a master/slave configuration, the slave database is already loaded and synchronizing. The result is that if the master goes down, the slave can take over very fast. This allows the database to react very fast on issues in the cluster. In an active/passive configuration, the procedure is a lot slower.

1. The cluster must detect that the active database is no longer responding.

2. If the entire node hosting the active database is no longer responding, the node has to be fenced.

3. The database has to load on the other cluster node.

In the sample cluster discussed here, an OCFS2 file system is used. Note that this is not a real requirement for active/passive database configurations, but the customer had a strong preference for a clones OCFS2 file system. There is also a benefit in such a configuration.

If a cluster is created in which an Ext4 or XFS file system is a part of the cluster resource, the risk of corruption is higher. Such a corruption may arise when node2 thinks that node1 is down, sends a STONITH to that node, STONITH fails, but resources are migrated anyway. True, it's not an extremely likely scenario, but a scenario that is real enough to consider. (In fact, I have seen such a scenario occurring, not because STONITH was failing, but because the administrator of the cluster made a stupid error.) If such a situation arises, you may end up with two databases, both writing to the same file system, without being aware of that. The result in the end is that the file system will be corrupted. To ensure that this would never happen, in this case, an OCFS2 file system was used.

The interesting part in the configuration of this cluster is in the dependencies of the resources that are different in nature. First, there is the ocfs2-base-group resource, which takes care of loading dlm and o2cb (the prerequisites for any OCFSs file system). Next, there is the ocfs2-base-clone, which can only load once the ocfs2-base-group resource has been loaded. And only when the ocfs2-base-clone has been loaded successfully, can the pgsql-group be loaded. The only way to make sure that this is occurring correctly is by using order constraints.

First, an order constraint is needed to load the OCFS2 file system after the ocfs2-base-group. Next, an order constraint is defined between the pgsql-group and the ocfs2-file-system. Note that in Listing 11-1, this second constraint is missing. (That's what happens when talking about real-life configurations, which offer a nice opportunity for new contact with the customer.)

Mail Front End

As mentioned previously, the mail front end has to support the round-robin Domain Name System (DNS) load balancing (which has nothing to do with the rest of this cluster). For that reason, floating IP addresses are defined. In this cluster, Internet Message Access Protocol (IMAP) services and Simple Mail Transfer Protocol (SMTP) services are provided. The idea is that the SMTP services have a preference for two specific nodes in the cluster, and the IMAP services have a preference for two other specific nodes in this cluster. To accomplish this, you can see that several constraints are used in this cluster.

The interesting part of this cluster is in the floating IP addresses. The SMTP addresses for the SMTP servers can run on either the smtp-1 or the smtp-2 hosts, and the addresses for the IMAP servers can run on imap-1 or imap-2. Note that the score that is used in these constraints is only set to 1,000. This score ensures that if both SMTP servers are down, the IP address will still be serviced by the IMAP servers.

The SMTP service also plays an important role in this cluster. It has to be started twice, once on each SMTP node. This is accomplished by putting the primitive in a clone resource that has a location constraint that is set with a score of -inf, which means never, to run on the IMAP servers. In Listing 11-2, you can see the complete configuration for this mail front-end cluster.

Listing 11-2. Use Case Mail Front-End Cluster

```
chimay:~ # cat cluster-santnet-4node-extern.conf
node imap-1.msexample.com
node imap-2.msexample.com
node smtp-1.msexample.com
node smtp-2.msexample.com
```

```
primitive ip-smtp-1 ocf:heartbeat:IPaddr2 \
        params ip="194.0.153.51" cidr_netmask="24" \
        op stop interval="0" timeout="20s" \
        op monitor interval="10s" timeout="20s" \
        op start interval="0" timeout="20s" \
        meta target-role="Started"
primitive ip-smtp-2 ocf:heartbeat:IPaddr2 \
        params ip="194.0.153.52" cidr_netmask="24" \
        op stop interval="0" timeout="20s" \
        op monitor interval="10s" timeout="20s" \
        op start interval="0" timeout="20s" \
        meta target-role="Started"
primitive ip-imap-1 ocf:heartbeat:IPaddr2 \
        params ip="194.0.153.53" cidr_netmask="24" \
        op stop interval="0" timeout="20s" \
        op monitor interval="10s" timeout="20s" \
        op start interval="0" timeout="20s" \
        meta target-role="Started"
primitive ip-imap-2 ocf:heartbeat:IPaddr2 \
        params ip="194.0.153.54" cidr_netmask="24" \
        op stop interval="0" timeout="20s" \
        op monitor interval="10s" timeout="20s" \
        op start interval="0" timeout="20s" \
        meta target-role="Started"
primitive service-postfix-1 ocf:heartbeat:postfix \
        op stop interval="0" timeout="60" \
        op start interval="0" timeout="60" \
        op monitor interval="20" timeout="40" \
        meta target-role="Started"
primitive stonith-vmkvm-imap-1 stonith:external/libvirt \
        params hostlist="imap-1.msexample.com" hypervisor_uri="qemu+ssh://192.168.50.254/system" \
        op monitor interval="60" timeout="20" start-delay="15" \
        op stop interval="0" timeout="15" \
        op start interval="0" timeout="20" \
        meta target-role="Started"
primitive stonith-vmkvm-imap-2 stonith:external/libvirt \
        params hostlist="imap-2.msexample.com" hypervisor_uri="qemu+ssh://192.168.50.254/system" \
        op monitor interval="60" timeout="20" start-delay="15" \
        op stop interval="0" timeout="15" \
        op start interval="0" timeout="20" \
        meta target-role="Started"
primitive stonith-vmkvm-smtp-1 stonith:external/libvirt \
        params hostlist="smtp-1.msexample.com" hypervisor_uri="qemu+ssh://192.168.50.254/system" \
        op monitor interval="60" timeout="20" start-delay="15" \
        op stop interval="0" timeout="15" \
        op start interval="0" timeout="20" \
        meta target-role="Started"
```

```
primitive stonith-vmkvm-smtp-2 stonith:external/libvirt \
        params hostlist="smtp-2.msexample.com" hypervisor_uri="qemu+ssh://192.168.50.254/system" \
        op monitor interval="60" timeout="20" start-delay="15" \
        op stop interval="0" timeout="15" \
        op start interval="0" timeout="20" \
        meta target-role="Started"
clone smtp-clone service-postfix-1 \
        meta clone-max="2" target-role="Started" clone-node-max="1"
location clone-postfix-loc smtp-clone \
        rule $id="clone-postfix-loc-rule" -inf: #uname eq imap-2.msexample.com or #uname eq
imap-1.msexample.com
location fence-imap-1 stonith-vmkvm-imap-1 -inf: imap-1.msexample.com
location fence-imap-2 stonith-vmkvm-imap-2 -inf: imap-2.msexample.com
location fence-smtp-1 stonith-vmkvm-smtp-1 -inf: smtp-1.msexample.com
location fence-smtp-2 stonith-vmkvm-smtp-2 -inf: smtp-2.msexample.com
location ip-imap-1-loc ip-imap-1 \
        rule $id="ip-imap-1-loc-rule" 1000: #uname eq imap-1.msexample.com or #uname eq
imap-2.msexample.com
location ip-imap-2-loc ip-imap-2 \
        rule $id="ip-imap-2-loc-rule" 1000: #uname eq imap-2.msexample.com or #uname eq
imap-1.msexample.com
location ip-smtp-1-loc ip-smtp-1 \
        rule $id="ip-smtp-1-loc-rule" 1000: #uname eq smtp-1.msexample.com or #uname eq
smtp-2.msexample.com
location ip-smtp-2-loc ip-smtp-2 \
        rule $id="ip-smtp-2-loc-rule" 1000: #uname eq smtp-2.msexample.com or #uname eq
smtp-1.msexample.com
property $id="cib-bootstrap-options" \
        dc-version="1.1.6-b988976485d15cb702c9307df55512d323831a5e" \
        cluster-infrastructure="openais" \
        expected-quorum-votes="4" \
        stonith-action="poweroff" \
        last-lrm-refresh="1391077071"
```

One Big Cluster or Many Little Clusters?

A question that has arisen while creating this solution is which approach to take. Two different solutions are possible. It's an option to create one big cluster, with a total of 14 hosts in this case, that are trying to take care of all services. In this environment, I selected the solution with many clusters communicating with one another.

To determine whether you need one big cluster or many little clusters, it is important to gauge dependency relations between services. If there are complex dependency relations, and you want to move resources if some depending resources are failing, it makes sense to put them all in one big cluster. This wasn't the case in this configuration. Communications between the mail front-end cluster and the database back-end cluster was simply based on IP address, and no other dependencies had to be defined. That is why in this solution, a configuration was created with many small clusters. Such a configuration has the advantage of making it relatively easy to focus on specific problems. Should one big cluster have been created, the need for complex constraints, defining relations between resources, would have been much bigger. This would also have resulted in it being more difficult to get an overview of resources in the cluster.

Summary

In this chapter, you have read how Pacemaker can be used to create a complex configuration, where multiple clusters are working together to create one big solution, where everything is highly available. As IT solutions tend to become more complicated, resolutions such as this are becoming more common. If a configuration is required in which multiple nodes have to work together to provide a solution that is highly available, the approach of creating multiple clusters that communicate with one another is preferable to a solution in which one big cluster tries to host all. By using several independent clusters, management is made easier.

Index

Get the eBook for only $10!

Now you can take the weightless companion with you anywhere, anytime. Your purchase of this book entitles you to 3 electronic versions for only $10.

This Apress title will prove so indispensible that you'll want to carry it with you everywhere, which is why we are offering the eBook in 3 formats for only $10 if you have already purchased the print book.

Convenient and fully searchable, the PDF version enables you to easily find and copy code—or perform examples by quickly toggling between instructions and applications. The MOBI format is ideal for your Kindle, while the ePUB can be utilized on a variety of mobile devices.

Go to www.apress.com/promo/tendollars to purchase your companion eBook.